Mustang
1964½-2003

Peter C. Sessler

MBI Publishing Company

First published in 2002 by MBI Publishing Company, Galtier Plaza, Suite 200, 380 Jackson Street, St. Paul, MN 55101-3885 USA

© Peter C. Sessler, 2002

All rights reserved. With the exception of quoting brief passages for the purposes of review, no part of this publication may be reproduced without prior written permission from the Publisher.

The information in this book is true and complete to the best of our knowledge. All recommendations are made without any guarantee on the part of the author or Publisher, who also disclaim any liability incurred in connection with the use of this data or specific details.

We recognize that some words, model names and designations, for example, mentioned herein are the property of the trademark holder. We use them for identification purposes only. This is not an official publication.

MBI Publishing Company books are also available at discounts in bulk quantity for industrial or sales-promotional use. For details write to Special Sales Manager at Motorbooks International Wholesalers & Distributors, Galtier Plaza, Suite 200, 380 Jackson Street, St. Paul, MN 55101-3885 USA.

Library of Congress Cataloging-in-Publication Data Available

ISBN 0-7603-1373-3

On the front cover: A 2003 SVT Mustang. *Ford Motor Co.*

On the back cover: A 2002 Mustang GT

Author Bio: Peter C. Sessler has been writing automotive books for over 20 years and has written 36 books. He has served as Editor-in-Chief for *MuscleCars* magazine and has an avid interest in cars. He has restored a Boss 429, a Shelby Cobra GT350 Convertible, as well as other models. He lives in Milford, Pennsylvania.

Printed in the United States of America

Contents

	Acknowledgments	*5*
	Introduction	*7*
	Investment ratings	*10*
1	1956 Mustangs	*11*
2	1966 Mustangs	*23*
3	1967 Mustangs	*29*
4	1968 Mustangs	*37*
5	1969 Mustangs	*45*
6	1970 Mustangs	*67*
7	1971–72 Mustangs	*83*
8	1973 Mustangs	*101*
9	1974–78 Mustang IIs	*105*
10	1979–89 Mustangs	*116*
11	1990–93 Mustangs	*137*
12	1994–95 Mustangs	*146*
13	1965–82 Shelby Mustangs	*153*
14	1996–1998 Mustangs	*194*
15	1999–2003 Mustangs	*201*

Appendices

Production Figures	*211*
Mustang Engines 1956–2003	*215*
High Performance Mustang Engines	*218*
Specifications	*223*
Clubs	*223*
Index	*224*

Acknowledgments

The author gratefully acknowledges the following Mustang enthusiasts who provided assistance by allowing their cars to appear in this book.

1965
Fred Agnoni—1965 convertible
Dennis Brooks—1965 2+2
Robert Curk—1965 2+2
Edward Ponsier—1965 GT convertible
Pete McManus—1965 GT 2+2
Alan Bolte—1965 GT350 R
Rick Zappia—1965 GT350
Brent Galloway—1965 GT350

1966
Carol Padden—1966 GT350H
Charles Bond—1966 GT 2+2
Mickey Standridge—1966 GT 2+2
Gary Hanson—1966 T-5
Rick Mitchell—1966 Sprint 200
Michael Barnett—1966 hardtop
Rick Kopec—1966 GT350
Carl Kubincanek—1966 GT350
Cliff Hornback—1966 GT350 convertible
Greg Kolasa—1966 GT350H
Roy Simkins—1966 GT350H

1967
Dane—1967 GT convertible
Charles Reichert—1967 GT convertible
Steve Woodward—1967 GT fastback
Dave Mathews—1967 GT350
Rick Zappia—1967 GT500 (427)

1968
Bob Burdette—1968 GT fastback
Perry Rivers—1968 GT convertible
George Wahl—1968½ Cobra Jet fastback
Rex Hall—1968½ Cobra Jet hardtop
Clay Holland—1968 California Special
Michael Leslie—1968 GT500KR convertible
Richard Kirshy—1968 GT500KR

1969
Van T. Read—1969 GT convertible
James Sherfesee—1969 GT SportsRoof
Brian Torres—1969 GT SportsRoof
Chris Herrel—1969 Mach 1
Bob Stanworth—1969 Mach 1
Kevin Zehr—1969 Mach 1
Randy Ream—1969 Boss 302
Ralph Surface—1969 Boss 429
Don Miller—1969 GT500
Ron Paulhamus—1969 GT500 convertible
John Slog—1969 GT350 convertible
John Christoffsen—1969 GT500

1970
Terry Fritts—1970 Twister
Trudy Kent-Montalbano—1970 Grabber SportsRoof
Bill Eybers—1970 Mach 1
Eugene Kennedy—1970 Mach 1
Dan Kiefer III—1970 Boss 302
Alec Garden—1970 Boss 302
Steve Dowdall—1970 Boss 429
Dane Miller—1970 Boss 429
Dave Mathews—1970 GT350 convertible

1971
Art Hubner—1971 Mach 1
Craig Comjean—1971 Mach 1 429SCJ-R
Perry Rushing—1971 Mach 1 429CJ-R
Marvin Scothorn—1971 Mach 1 429SCJ-R

1972
Paul McLaughlin—1972 SportsRoof
Daniel V. Zakarian—1972 HO
Jerry Holiber—1972 Sprint convertible

1973
Charlene Galloway—1973 Mach 1

1976
Joy Jacobs—Cobra II

1978
Gary Baum—Mach 1
Dale Rabe—King Cobra
Antoinette Schulberger—King Cobra

1979-89

Jerry Umstead—1982 GT
Steven Jacobs—1984 20th Anniversary three-door
Glen Trincone—1984 20th Anniversary convertible
Jack Benson—1987 GT three-door

Special thanks to Brent Galloway, Rick Kopec, Vinnie Liska, Frank McIntyre, Paul McLaughlin, Randy Ream, Bobby Spedale, Jim Wicks, Rick Zappia and Paul Postelnicu.

Introduction

Much has happened to the Mustang since the original edition of this book was written. The first Mustang buyer's guide focused exclusively on the first-generation performance Mustangs: the GTs, the Bosses, the Mach 1s and, of course, the Shelby Mustangs. Interest in these cars is as strong as, if not stronger than, ever but many enthusiasts are finding that the less glamorous Mustangs are indeed collectible and much less expensive to acquire. At the same time, the second-generation Mustangs are beginning to show some signs of life after years of being put down because they shared many parts with the Pinto. Third-generation Mustangs have finally come into their own, especially from a performance point of view, and although they may not be considered a collectible now, they are popular and do have a strong following.

You may ask, can a car that was built in the millions have any collector value at all? The performance Mustangs, even though they have traditionally received all the hype and promotion, were never built in great numbers, and indeed, most of these Mustangs are appreciating collectibles. Properly optioned-out regular Mustangs, particularly convertibles and some of the fastbacks, can squeak into the collector category, but the great mass of nonperformance Mustangs just don't have true collector value. That doesn't mean that you can't spend a lot of money restoring or acquiring such cars; you can, but I don't think you should place such a Mustang in the same league as a Boss 302 or any Shelby. You can spend just as much restoring a 1966 six-cylinder notchback or a 1966 GT convertible. Obviously, the GT convertible is a better investment. The point is that Mustangs that don't have collector status should be acquired with the idea that these cars are really meant to be enjoyed—and should definitely not be gotten with the idea that in a few years you're going to double your investment.

It is important that you take the time to get an idea of what Mustangs are selling for. Publications such as *Hemmings Motor News*, *Old Cars Price Guide* and the want ads columns of Mustang club newsletters are a good source. Lately, you'll see asking prices all over the place, especially for Mustangs that don't really have the historical significance and rarity to warrant such prices. You have to be discriminating, but just as important, you have to decide which Mustang you are interested in.

Mustangs were built to appeal to a more youthful buyer than the typical Ford customer of the mid-sixties. It has been said that you can sell a young man's car to an old man, but you can't sell an old man's car to a young man. The Mustang, with its long option list (which got longer as the years went on) was designed to appeal to diverse groups of buyers, but the youth factor was always an important ingredient. The Mustang's long option list made it a car for all people, but today, for the prospective Mustang collector, this variety can be a nightmare. *Illustrated Mustang Buyer's Guide* will help you wade through the options.

If you have the Mustang bug, you can look in the publications mentioned earlier to see what is available, but your best bet, at least initially, is to go to some Mustang shows. Most Mustang shows are held from early spring to late fall. *Mustang Monthly* magazine publishes a good list of upcoming events as does *Hemmings*. Going to a show is fun and educational. You'll see a lot of different Mustangs, and there is nothing like seeing the cars and colors in person. You'll find that most Mustang owners are more than happy to talk to you (and sometimes at great length!) about their cars. But you also have to be cautious because much information in circulation is simply wrong.

Joining a local club is a good idea as is joining one of the national clubs.

If you think you have found the Mustang of your dreams, the first and most important thing to do is to inspect it for rust. Mustangs, and most cars built in the 1960s and 1970s, are prone to rust. Rear quarter panels and front fenders are the most obvious places to look, but rocker panels, trunk, floors and doors are all susceptible to rust. If you know the Mustang you are looking at has had substantial body work, inspect it on a lift and also look at the condition of the floors. Like all unibody cars, a severely rusted Mustang is not worth restoring.

The important thing is to take your time. It can be hard to be objective if your heart is beating fast, hands are sweating and you stutter every other word! Just slow down if you are excited; otherwise you are going to miss seeing imperfections. Take the car for a drive to make sure that everything works—just as you would any new car—and note anything that doesn't sound right. Have the owner drive the car while you follow behind. You'll be able to see any telltale puffs of smoke which can indicate engine problems.

If you see any imperfections or problem areas, let the seller know you are aware of them. Like other sellers, a Mustang owner always asks more than what he is willing to take. If you can't come to a satisfactory price, don't worry. Ford made a lot of Mustangs, and it shouldn't be too difficult to locate another.

I also recommend that you buy a car that is as complete as possible and as restored as possible. You'll always underestimate the cost of a restoration because, once you start, the tendency is to try to build a brand new car, replacing parts that may not need to be replaced. Also, a good, solid low-mileage original Mustang is more desirable than a restoration loaded with reproduction parts. These original cars, of course, are hard to find but expect to pay a premium for one.

During the past ten years, companies and individuals producing reproduction parts have mushroomed—a boon for the Mustang enthusiast. The only criticism I have heard is that this can take the challenge out of restoring a Mustang; all you have to do is call a few toll-free numbers. Still, the quicker your restoration is finished, the sooner you'll be enjoying your Mustang.

Another point to consider is originality. Rare, low-production Mustangs are definitely worth more if kept in original condition. Modified Mustangs, unless modified with factory- or dealer-installed options, such as the Cobra kits, are not considered within the bounds of originality. It is hard, however, to keep these cars strictly original. For example, the addition of radial tires will improve the ride and handling of any Mustang but they were not always stock equipment.

My advice on originality is to go ahead and modify the car if it makes driving it more enjoyable. I would, however, keep all the original parts. As long as the Mustang can easily be reconverted when it comes time to part with it, modifications should not hurt its value.

Of course, such a car would not score well in a concours show where originality is paramount. In this type of show, the car has to be in exactly the same condition as it was the day it left the factory. Such cars are rarely driven, and some enthusiasts feel that part of the fun of owning a Mustang is driving it, especially the hot high-performance models.

With any Mustang, it is best to get one that has more options. Naturally, some

Mustangs had few options, such as the Boss 429, but with others, the more options the better. For example, the 1969 Mach 1 did not have power steering and power brakes standard. The 428CJ Mach 1 equipped with manual steering and manual drum brakes is definately not the way to go with such a powerful car. More options mean greater value and better driving pleasure.

I treat each year of the first generation Mustangs, from 1965 through 1973, in one chapter, with the excaption of the 1971–72 Mustangs which are combined in a single chapter. Second-generation Mustangs, those built from 1974 through 1978, are covered in one chapter. These Mustangs aren't in the same league as the first-generation cars, but they do have a solid core of support. And some Mustangs built in those years are worth considering. Third-generation Mustangs, 1979 through 1993, are also covered in two chapters. All through the seventies and early eighties, we've been told how the current Mustangs don't compare with the originals. Well, the third-generation Mustangs, particularly the GTs built from 1985 to 2003, can stand on their own and offer exceptional performance and handling.

I have not included a price guide in this edition because it would quickly become out of date. Your best bet is to look in *Hemmings* and other publications.

Occasionally, you may run into a Mustang that doesn't quite fit published specifications in terms of optional equipment or color. Remember, you could order Mustangs in colors other than those listed—such cars had no color code on the data plate. And it is possible to have Mustangs equipped with options or in combinations that don't normally occur, the result of a special order or manufacturing errors. If you find such a car and are interested in it, make sure of its history and authenticity.

The Mustang created great excitement when it was first introduced. There have been other pony cars, but the Mustang was the original—it still has that special magic. Whether you buy one as an investment, a restoration project or simply to drive and enjoy, you'll find that it is a rewarding experience.

Peter C. Sessler *July, 1995*
Milford, PA

Investment ratings

★★★★★ These are the highest priced, rarest and most sought after of all Mustangs. These special Mustangs will continue to appreciate at a faster pace in the coming years than will other Mustangs.

★★★★ Still rare and desirable, the Mustangs in this category are solid investments and, fortunately, more numerous. Cars in this category have true collector status and thus can be considered a good investment.

★★★ Lower priced and more numerous, these Mustangs lack the breeding of four- and five-star cars. A three-star car is a good entry level Mustang that may possibly have future potential, depending on color, options and production.

★★ These cars represent a relatively economical way to participate in the hobby. Don't expect these Mustangs to appreciate much because they just aren't considered special enough. Their value will invariably be linked to that of other higher priced Mustangs.

★ This category includes Mustangs that just don't have much collector interest or potential. Mustangs without the original engine size and type, highly modified Mustangs and severe basket cases are also one-star cars.

Without exception, it is the high-performance Mustangs, Shelbys, Bosses, Mach 1s and GTs that are the most desirable and collectible—no matter what category of star rating they happen to fall into. For example, a 1966 GT convertible will be worth more than a plain 1966 convertible, even if both cars have the same options.

Because so many Mustangs have been built and in so many guises, I have been frugal in giving out four and five stars. These Mustangs have to be truly special and must satisfy the following criteria: low production, historical significance and uniqueness. You really need all three criteria. There are many Mustangs that were built in fairly low numbers, for example, those with oddball option combinations, but keep in mind that low production by itself is not enough.

Four- and five-star Mustangs should come with documentation. You should be able to trace their history—and all the better if the car comes with original paperwork, such as the window sticker and dealer sales receipts. I know of one enthusiast who has even found out the name of the salesman who originally sold the car! Be suspect of a Mustang that is missing the warranty plate or sticker and the complimentary underhood build tag. Remember too that the Boss 302 and Boss 429 Mustangs also had the serial number of the car inscribed on the engine, something that was not done on other Mustangs.

As Mustangs become more valuable and more collectible in the coming years, the temptation to pass off fakes as originals will increase too.

Finally, make sure you insure your Mustang with a reputable insurer for stated value. There are specialty insurers (look in *Hemmings*) for collector cars. Don't assume that your local insurance agent knows that your Mustang is a valuable collectible.

Chapter 1

1965 Mustangs

★★	1965 Hardtop
★★✦	1965 Fastback
★★★	1965 Convertible
Add ★	1965 GT with K code 289 V-8

Few people were disappointed when the Mustang finally went on sale on April 17, 1964. It was, and still is, Ford Motor Company's most successful and exciting car built since World War II. The Mustang just happened to be introduced at the right time, yet its success would not have been assured if it had been a mediocre product. It was a reasonably well-built car, boasted great styling, and with its long option list and three body styles, it was designed to appeal to as many buyers as possible.

All Mustangs built between March 1964 and early August 1965 were titled and coded as 1965 models. Thus, while there is no such thing as a 1964½ model, there are differences between those built before August 1964 (referred to as 1964½s or early 1965s) and those that came after. You will, however, find late 1965 Mustangs with parts and features that supposedly were only available on the 1964½ versions. Production changes often occur during the model year, and a manufacturer will almost always use up the

The ultimate 1965 Mustang was a GT convertible. This fine example also has the optional styled steel wheels.

11

The 1965 convertible looks even better with the top down. GT Mustangs of 1965 did not have any side ornamentation on the rear quarter panels.

The most distinctive features of the Mustang GT were the grille-mounted foglamps.

existing stock of a part before switching over to its successor.

The Mustang was initially offered in a hardtop and a convertible. The fastback, or 2+2 as it was called, was not introduced until September 1964. The 2+2 really added to the Mustang's magic. The Mustang continued to be available in these three body styles until the 1973 model year.

In part, the Mustang was so successful because of its pricing. A two-door hardtop had a suggested retail price of $2,320.86. For that you got a 170 ci six-cylinder engine rated at 101 hp mated to a three-speed manual transmission with a floor shifter; in fact, all Mustangs have floor-mounted shifters. Manual steering with a slow 27:1 ratio and manual drum brakes measuring nine inches were standard. Standard tires were blackwall 6.50×13 mounted on four-lug thirteen-inch rims (on V-8s, fourteen-inch rims replaced the thirteen inchers after September 1964). Obviously, such a Mustang would not be much fun to drive.

Front suspension was independent, with coil springs mounted over the upper A-arm. Rear suspension was a solid axle on leaf springs; basic but dependable.

Dual exhausts with these distinctive outlets were also part of the GT package.

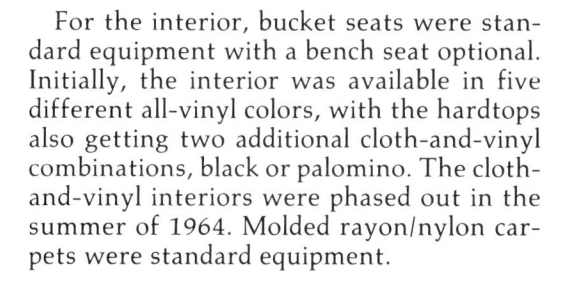

All 1965 GTs came with front fender emblems and rocker panel stripes.

For the interior, bucket seats were standard equipment with a bench seat optional. Initially, the interior was available in five different all-vinyl colors, with the hardtops also getting two additional cloth-and-vinyl combinations, black or palomino. The cloth-and-vinyl interiors were phased out in the summer of 1964. Molded rayon/nylon carpets were standard equipment.

The Mustang in standard form provided just the basics of transportation in a pleasing body. The prospective customer was offered and encouraged to personalize his or her Mustang with a large and ever increasing selection of options.

The 170 ci six-cylinder with its anemic performance was replaced by a larger 200 ci six in the fall of 1964. Both were based on the original 144 ci six that powered the 1960

1965 GT 2+2 fastback. *Pete McManus*

The 1965 2+2 accentuated the Mustang's youthful, sporty image. The Mustang fastback was also visually more satisfying than other Detroit fastbacks of the mid-1960s era.

All 1965 Mustangs came with vertical and horizontal grille bars. This example has the stock wheel covers.

Falcon. The 200 featured seven main bearings (four were used on the 144 and 170) that provided additional strength. The 200 ci six continued as the standard Mustang engine until 1970.

One of the problems with this engine, at least from a performance point of view, was harmonic vibration. Vibrations travel from the front of the crankshaft to the flywheel where they are returned to the front of the crank. This is normal with all engines. The problem with the 200 was that it did not have a vibration dampener to absorb the vibrations, so the bearings, timing gears and even the flywheel could break when the engine was over-revved. And the design of the integral intake manifold/head severely limited engine breathing. However, provided you didn't over-rev the 200, it was a hard engine to kill.

To provide more pep, a 164 hp 260 ci V-8 and a 210 hp 289 ci V-8 were optional. The

The spare tire took a good part of the trunk space.

271 hp 289 was available after June 1, 1964. By fall, the 260 was replaced with a two-barrel version of the 289 rated at 200 hp,

The interior could accommodate four in reasonable comfort. This GT convertible has a console and the optional Rally-Pac. Note the five-gauge instrument cluster.

15

Close-up of Rally-Pac. Many versions were available depending on the engine; a Rally-Pac could have been factory- or dealer-installed and could be dated early or late 1965.

This interior shows the standard instrument cluster.

while the four-barrel was now rated at 225 hp. Although the 225 hp Challenger 289 provided adequate performance with 0-60 mph times in the 8.5 second range and quarter-mile times of about 16.5 seconds, it could not be considered high-performance. For more power and acceleration, the 271 hp 289 ci V-8 was the way to go.

The 289 was one of Ford's best engines. The engine family was originally designed in 1958 as an answer to Chevrolet's highly successful small-block. It did not come into production until 1961, and then with only 221 ci. Not particularly successful, it was enlarged to 260 and then to 289 ci. Unlike earlier Ford engines, this was a compact, light engine, weighing about 450 pounds complete. It featured lightweight thin-wall casting techniques, and with its 4.00×2.87 inch bore and stroke, it was conducive to high rpm operation. The basic engine survived and is still in production today.

The 271 hp engine had a larger 480 cfm Autolite carburetor, versus the 470 cfm unit found on the 225 hp 289. A higher compression ratio of 10.5:1 and a performance dual-

The air conditioner hung below the dash as on this convertible.

point distributor further distinguished it. Internally, the engine used a mechanical camshaft that enabled it to rev higher and produce more power. To ensure reliability at higher rpm, the 271 hp 289 had screw-in rocker arm studs, special connecting rods with larger, stronger ⅜ inch rod bolts and a special harmonic balancer. The balancer, two inches wide versus one inch for other 289s, was designed to operate at engine speeds up to 7000 rpm. A low-restriction air cleaner topped off the engine and added some distinction. A low-restriction dual exhaust system let all know that this was a special Mustang. Ford rated it at 271 hp at 6000 rpm, but that was based on a gross rating. Measured by today's net rating, actual power was closer to 230–235 hp.

Mandatory with this engine was a four-speed manual transmission with either a 3.89:1 or 4.11:1 axle ratio in the larger nine-

The fold-down rear seat was a useful option on the 2+2.

You can recognize the Interior Decor Group option by the embossed ponies on the seat upholstery. Most Mustang enthusiasts refer to this option as the pony interior.

inch rear. The letter K designated the 271 hp 289 ci engine on the Mustang's data plate.

The 271 hp engine improved acceleration dramatically: 0–60 mph times in the mid-seven-second range and quarter-mile times in the high fifteens. Although these figures do not seem that impressive, the subjective feeling was that this car was much faster than it really was. The high numerical axle ratio made this Mustang responsive and eager to accelerate. Downshifting and flooring it at the same time brought about considerable sensory input: you were pushed back into your seat as the nose of the car rose about six inches, while the engine screamed and the tires more often than not broke traction.

Included with the 271 hp engine was the special handling package that included stiffer springs and shocks, as well as fourteen-inch tires and wheels. Optional with the V-8s and suspension package were 5.90×15 Firestone Super Sport tires, but these were replaced with 6.95×14s by the fall of 1964.

The automatic transmission was not available with the K engine, but it was available on all other Mustang engines, as was a four-speed manual, in place of the standard three-speed manual. Other important options included power brakes, manual front

The standard engine on the 1964½ Mustangs was this 170 ci six-cylinder.

disc brakes, power steering with a faster 22:1 ratio, limited-slip differential, styled steel wheels, underdash air-conditioning and Rally-Pac. The Rally-Pac combined a clock and tachometer which were mounted on the steering column. Many other trim and functional options were available, plus a host of dealer-installed options.

Two significant options were made available in 1965. The first was the Interior Decor Group, introduced in March 1965. It was essentially a luxury interior option with deluxe door panels, special seat upholstery with galloping pony inserts, woodgrain steering wheel, woodgrain appliques on the glovebox door, and a special five-dial instrument cluster, as well as some other trim differences. The all-important letter B indicated the Interior Decor Group on the bodyside code on the warranty plate. Thus in 1965, the designations 65B, 63B and 76B indicated the luxury interior, while the standard interior had the letter A. The pony interior, as the luxury option was commonly called, did spruce up the inside.

The other option was the GT Equipment Group. Available on all three body styles, the GT group enhanced the Mustang's appearance and also improved performance. It was available with either the 225 hp or 271 hp 289s, and it included manual front disc brakes, handling package, quick-ratio steering, dual exhaust with chrome exhaust trumpets exiting through the rear valance panel, rocker panel stripes, GT emblems and two foglamps on each end of the grille opening.

Inside, the standard instrument bezel was replaced with the five-dial version that housed gauges for fuel, temperature, speed, oil pressure and amps. GTs equipped with the pony interior got the same five-dial bezel, but with the walnut trim. Later in the model year, Ford made available the appearance items as dealer-installed accessories. Al-

More common was one of the Challenger 289s.

though the styled steel wheels and Rally-Pac were not part of the GT Equipment Group, they do complement it and are popular add-ons today.

True GTs were built from February 1965 through August 1965 and must have date codes from P through V on the warranty plates. Besides the date code on the warranty plate, other differences distinguish early 1965 Mustangs from later ones. The most obvious difference on the early 1965s is the use of a generator, while Mustangs built after August used an alternator; wiring is different for each of these. The 170 ci six-cylinder engine was only available on the early cars. The passenger seat was not adjustable (although you'll find later Mustangs may also have this type of seat). On later cars, allen screws hold on window cranks and door handles. Early cars have a two-speed blower versus a three-speed on later cars. A host of other minor differences exist as well.

Compared to today's Mustangs, the 1965 is dated in some respects, but overall, you'll find that you can drive the car everyday. The seats do not offer much lateral support and do not have any rake adjustment, and the steering wheel is a bit on the large side. The dash is simple, and you don't need a college degree to figure out how everything works. The heating and air-conditioning systems work just fine, but you will notice that there is more interior noise at speed and that the radio leaves a lot to be desired. However, you'll be surprised how nicely and smoothly the engine idles and how responsive it is. The power steering is light but unfortunately does not convey much road feel. Of course, you'll also be noticed more in a 1965, especially in a convertible.

Specials
Indianapolis Pace Car

The rarest 1965 Mustangs were the Indianapolis 500 Pace Cars. Two 1964½ convert-

The ultimate 289 was this 271 hp version. Mustangs powered by this engine are frequently referred to as K cars, as this engine used the letter K in the VIN.

ibles were used in the race itself—one as the official pace car and the other as a back-up car. In addition, thirty-five convertibles were given to the Indianapolis 500 dignitaries and Festival board of directors. All were powered by 289s, but the two Pace Cars came with the High Performance 289 and Borg Warner transmissions. All Pace Cars were painted Pace Car White, which was different from the production Wimbledon White, and had either red, white or blue interiors. All these cars had the letter C as a color code—which also designated the color Honey Gold on 1965 Mustangs. Some of the Festival cars are still in existence, while the two cars used in the race wait to be found.

In addition, Ford built 185 Indianapolis Pace Car replica hardtops and gave them to Ford dealers as prizes in the Green and Checkered Flag Contests. All were equipped with the 260 ci V-8 and automatic transmission. They all were Pace Car White with a white and blue vinyl interior and had the Pace Car decals as well.

Any 1965 Mustang looked better with the optional styled steel wheels. These came with a red center cap.

Prospects

If you are considering restoring a Mustang be wary of rust. I don't think there is a part on these cars that doesn't rust. Doors, fenders, rear quarters, rocker panels, torque

Only a month after introduction, the Mustang was chosed for use in the Indianapolis 500. Ford Motor Company stock wheel covers with simulated knock-off spinners were optional on other Mustangs as well.

21

boxes, engine compartment, roof, floors—you name it, all are susceptible to rust. Naturally, if you can find an original car with no rust, all the better. If you are looking at a restoration, make sure that you inspect the car in question thoroughly. Rust damage repaired with Bondo means that the rust will return—and soon. Stay away from total rustbuckets. They simply aren't worth the effort.

Which Mustang should you get? A brief look at the production figures for 1965 Mustangs shows you that Ford built 680,989. Of these, 501,965 were hardtops. The sheer weight of these numbers suggests that prices for hardtops, at least in the near future, aren't going to go through the roof. If you are going to restore a 1965 Mustang and assuming the cost of parts and labor is the same for all three body styles, you are better off investing in a convertible or a fastback. You will see greater appreciation.

Although convertibles were built in greater numbers than were fastbacks, 101,945 versus 77,079, they are appreciating faster because of demand. The 1965 Mustang convertible is a classic design, and I think you'll see continued appreciation in spite of such high production.

Probably the most desirable 1965 would be a convertible GT with the 271 hp 289 and the pony interior, with such niceties as the styled steel wheels and Rally-Pac. GTs with the 225 hp Challenger are also quite desirable. I think a white or red Mustang is especially attractive. In any case, all 1965 Mustangs are beautiful and desirable, and I think that we can be thankful that for the most part they are still readily available (as far as collectibles go) and not very expensive.

1965–66 Mustang GT equipment
225 hp 289 ci V-8
Dual exhaust system with flared, chrome tailpipe extensions
Special Handling Package (heavy-duty springs and shocks, $^{13}/_{16}$ inch front sway bar, quick-ratio 22:1 steering)
Five-dial instrument cluster (fuel, temperature, speedometer, oil pressure, amperes)
Front disc brakes
Two 4 in. grille-mounted foglamps
Brightmetal hood accent molding
GT fender emblems
GT letters on gas filler cap
Racing stripe on lower body area
Desirable options
271 hp 289 ci V-8
4-speed manual or 3-speed automatic transmission
Rally-Pac
Styled steel wheels
Interior Decor Group (pony interior)
Console
Power brakes
Power steering

At least 185 Pace Car replica hardtops were built for use as dealer incentives. *Ford Motor Company*

22

Chapter 2

★★	1966 Hardtop
★★✓	1966 Fastback
★★★	1966 Convertible
Add ★	1966 GT with K code 289 V-8

1966 Mustangs

Why change a good thing? This was the basic rationale that Ford applied to the making of the 1966 Mustang, and production lines were humming, trying to keep up with all the demand. Clearly, the Mustang was a phenomenon, establishing a new niche in the marketplace and still enjoying no real competition. Chrysler's Barracuda never really caught on, and General Motors' answer to the Mustang, the Camaro and the Firebird, was still a good year away. Ford dealers were cleaning up.

Differing little from 1965 Mustangs, the 1966 Mustangs came with a little more standard trim. Most obvious were the rocker panel moldings and rear quarter ornamentation designed to simulate rear scoops.

23

As in 1965, the biggest seller were the notchbacks. This example has the optional wire wheel covers.

All 1966 Mustangs came with the five-pod instrument cluster on the dashboard, whether they were GTs or not.

The hardtop GT had a more formal look, yet had all the GT features.

A 1966 GT 2+2. GTs did not come with the rocker panel moldings. Optional styled steel wheels used a chrome trim ring.

Those of us who grew up in the sixties remember those years as an optimistic time. The Mustang with its fresh styling and spirited performance was the right car for a large group of people who found the typical Detroit sedan boring. The Mustang with its smaller dimensions and lighter weight felt like a nimble sports car in comparison.

The 1966 Mustang sold at a faster pace than had the record 1965: 607,568 units in twelve months versus 559,451 for the 1965, if you exclude the 1964 ½s.

The most noticeable change was the floating horse in the front grille, which gave the Mustang a cleaner look. On the sides, three chrome spires simulated a side scoop, but this ornament was deleted on the fastback and on all Mustangs that came with the GT package, as well as on those with the accent pinstripe. Other visual changes included standard rocker panel moldings (except on the fastback), a redesigned gas cap and standard back-up lights (optional on 1965 Mustangs). For the interior, different upholstery patterns and colors were available, but the most significant addition was the use of the five-dial instrument bezel across the board for both V-8 and six-cylinder Mustangs.

The standard wheel cover was redesigned, while the optional styled steel wheels used a chrome trim ring. Standard wheels were 14×4.5 inch (with four lugs) on six-cylinder Mustangs and 14×5 inch on V-8s. Tire size was 6.95×14.

The standard engine was the 200 ci six with the nonsynchromesh three-speed manual transmission. Optional were the 200 hp, 225 hp and 271 hp 289 ci V-8s as seen in 1965. The Cruise-O-Matic automatic transmission was an option with the 271 hp Cobra 289.

The GT Equipment Group was basically the same as the one offered in the 1965. The most obvious change was the use of a unique GT gas cap. The GTs, however, continued to use the horizontal grille bars, thereby closely resembling the 1965s.

Close-up of wire wheel cover.

Standard 200 cubic inch six-cylinder.

The optional 289 engine came in three horsepower versions. All 1966 Ford engines were painted blue.

The Interior Decor Group, too, remained practically unchanged. Again, for those so desiring, a front bench seat was optional on hardtops and convertibles, but not on fastbacks or any Mustang with the Interior Decor Group. Bench seats, although certainly rare, do not really contribute to a Mustang's value. They are more an interesting curiosity.

Specials
Sprint 200

To commemorate the one millionth Mustang sold, Ford released the Sprint 200 Option Group on the hardtop, convertible and fastback. It consisted of the 200 six-cylinder engine, wire wheel covers, pinstripes, center console and a chrome air cleaner with a Sprint 200 decal to dress up the engine compartment. The Sprint 200 Mustang was also a way for Ford to sell more six-cylinder Mustangs, as for a time, there was a shortage of 289 V-8 engines. Many magazine advertisements promoted the Sprint 200, most targeting young women—

1966 Sprint 200 hardtop. Hardtops were the most common, though convertibles and fastbacks were built as well. *Rick Mitchell*

for example, one lead line read "Six and the Single Girl."

The only way to tell a Sprint 200 from a regular Mustang was by the differences in equipment described above. Neither car had

T-5 Mustangs were destined for Germany; this is a 1966 GT. *Gary Hanson*

Note the full-length rocker panel stripe and T-5 emblems. *Gary Hanson*

Labeling Mustang T-5s for the German market continued well into the 1970s. *Gary Hanson*

any special code or VIN number. One way to tell is to see if the quarter panels were drilled open. The Sprint 200 did not come with the side ornamentation, and thus the attaching holes for it were never drilled open. If you think that you are looking at a Sprint 200, I suggest that you look at the quarter panel from the inside.

Also unique to 1966 was the T-5 Mustang. The name Mustang had already been used by a manufacturer in Germany, so Ford renamed all Mustangs destined for Germany T-5. All Mustang emblems were removed, and T-5 emblems were used on both front fenders. This practice continued to at least 1979.

Prospects

My recommendations for buying the 1966 Mustang are the same as those for the 1965s. GT convertibles lead the way, followed by GT fastbacks. Production of Mustangs equipped with the 271 hp 289 ci actually declined in 1966, thereby making these even more desirable.

As a group, the 1965-66 Mustangs represent the marque at its purest, but they are far from being rare. As for desirability, a slight edge goes to the 1965s simply because they were the first.

Chapter 3

1967 Mustangs

★★	1967 Hardtop
★★★	1967 Fastback
★★★	1967 Convertible
Add ★	1967 GT with K code 289 V-8
Add ★	1967 GT with 390 V-8

Fortunately, Ford restyled the Mustang in 1967. The Mustang, successful as it was, would have looked dated next to General Motors' entries in the pony car market, the Camaro and the Firebird. When the design for the 1967 Mustang was finalized in early 1965, Ford did not know exactly what GM's answer to the Mustang would be. The Cor-

The 1967 Mustang featured a much larger grille opening, giving the Mustang a meaner look.

29

The 1967 hardtop retained the same proportions, capitalizing on a successful theme. New side sculpturing gave the Mustang more of a racer look. This plain jane hardtop has the stock wheel covers.

The GT Mustangs were still the hottest production Mustangs. Most GT styling features were carried over from 1966. This is a GTA fastback.

Ford stylists again produced a successful design in 1967, this time a full fastback. Full fastbacks on anything larger than a car the size of the Mustang somehow lacked the proportional integrity, tending to look big and heavy.

vair clearly was no match, and it was obvious that GM would introduce something new, especially in light of the Mustang's incredible success.

Ford decided then to keep the styling similar to that of the successful original, while refining and improving the car. No one could mistake the 1967 for anything but a Mustang. It still looked like the original and retained the original's proportions, but it became a bit fuller and rounder. The grille opening was enlarged, and this gave the 1967 a meaner look. The 2+2 body, now a full fastback, looked sleeker than ever. All Mustangs got simulated scoops on the rear quarter panels, adding to the Mustang's performance image. The rear end treatment, still using three taillights per side, was very different. The taillight panel was concave, simulating the spoiled look found on Ford's GT40 endurance racers.

The wider track enabled Ford to improve the Mustang's ride and handling characteristics—a welcome improvement—while the enlarged engine compartment was now able to accommodate the big-block 390 ci V-8.

The change to a big block was a good thing because both GM pony cars were designed

Manual transmission GTs got the GT designation.

31

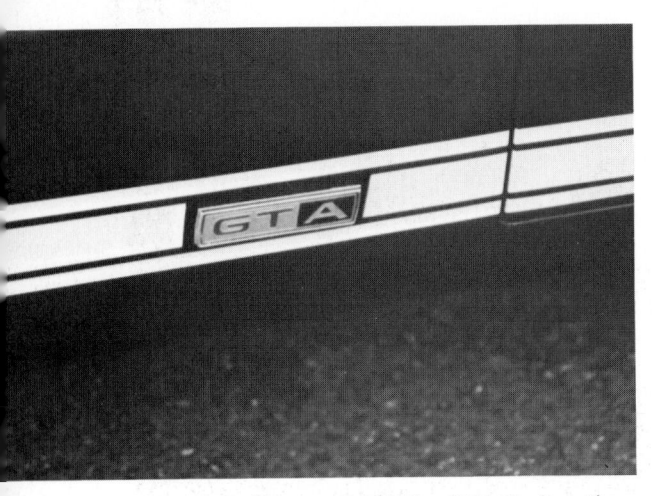

Automatic GTs came with the GTA designation.

from the beginning to accommodate big-block engines. The Camaro was available with several versions of the 396 ci V-8, the top version rated at 375 hp, while the Firebird could be had with a 325 hp 400 ci V-8. The muscle car war was heating up, and although the 289 was a good engine, it was no match for the big-blocks.

The 390 was a derivative of the FE series, originally introduced in Ford passenger cars in 1958. The 390 ci displacement first saw service in 1961. It was a physically large, heavy engine weighing over 700 pounds. With a relatively small bore and long stroke of 4.05×3.78 inches, it made a lot of low-end torque for excellent low-end performance. In the Mustang, the Thunderbird Special, as it was called, the 390 got an improved hydraulic camshaft (the same camshaft would later be used in the 428CJ/SCJ engines) and a 600 cfm Holley four-barrel carburetor. The 390 wasn't really a performance engine. Two-bolt mains, cast-iron crankshaft, restrictive manifolding and weak valve springs tended to reduce mid- and upper-rpm performance. Because of these deficiencies it ran out of breath at about 4000–4500 rpm. Still, acceleration with the 390 was faster than with any previous production Mustang. Typical 0–60 mph times were in the low-seven-second range, at least with a four-speed manual and high numerical rear axle gears. The 390 provided easy, smooth, unrestrained acceleration. A four-speed-equipped 390 with a high numerical rear axle ratio could reach the quarter-mile in about fifteen seconds.

The 1967 Mustang, with its revised front suspension and improved tires, handled better. Even though it still understeered, cornering limits were higher than before.

The 1967 Mustangs featured a more pronounced side scoop simulation. The optional styled steel wheels on this GT came with chrome trim rings and blue center caps.

Another new feature was the hood-mounted turn signal indicators.

Taillight panel treatment differed considerably from that on the 1965-66 Mustangs, although the three-taillight theme was carried over. Note the GT gas cap and quad exhaust outlets.

The 1967 interior featured a revised dash. This Mustang has the deluxe steering wheel and optional console.

The Interior Decor Group featured brushed aluminum door and dash panel inserts. The attractive steering wheel was owner-installed.

Unfortunately, with the 390, and its poor front-to-rear weight distribution, handling deteriorated, losing the nimbleness of 289 Mustangs. However, the 390 Mustang did not do so badly when compared with its competition.

Standard engine was the 200 ci six-cylinder with the three-speed manual. The only other transmission available with the six was a three-speed automatic. Three 289 V-8s were available: a two-barrel 200 hp, four-barrel 225 hp and appearing for the last time, the 271 hp High Performance 289 (but only with the GT Equipment Group). All these, except the 271 hp 289, came with a three-speed manual; a four-speed manual and automatic were options.

Other driveline improvements included a slightly faster manual steering ratio, 25.3:1

The biggest engine available in 1967 was the 390 GT rated at 320 hp. Chrome engine components (valve covers, air cleaner and oil filler cap) came with this husky engine. This one also had air conditioning.

(power 20.3:1), and new front disc brakes were available with power assist.

For the serious enthusiast, the Competition Handling Package was available at a cost of $388.53. High cost limited the popularity of this option as it was only available with the GT package. It included stiffened springs, Gabriel adjustable shocks, quick-ratio steering, a larger $^{15}/_{16}$ inch front sway bar, limited-slip axle with a minimum 3.25:1 ratio and fifteen-inch steel wheels with wire wheel covers. The package was a worthwhile addition with the big 390 engine.

Major option groups included the Interior Decor Group that did not include pony seat inserts and, of course, the GT Equipment Group, available only on V-8 Mustangs. It included grille-mounted foglamps, power front disc brakes, dual exhausts with chrome quad outlets (excluded with the 200 hp 289), rocker panel stripes with GT or GT/A (for automatic) emblem, F70×14 whitewall tires and GT pop-open gas cap, as well as a handling package with stiffer springs and shocks, and a larger front sway bar.

More common were the six-cylinder and the 289 V-8 (shown).

An Exterior Decor Group was also available for the first time. It included a hood with rear-facing louvers that also housed turn

A 1967 GT convertible not only looks great but is the most valuable 1967 Mustang.

The 1967 convertibles were the first to be equipped with a glass rear window.

signal indicators, wheelwell moldings, rear deck moldings on convertibles and hardtops, and a pop-open gas cap.

Other options and improvements included air conditioning with outlets built into the dash, convertible tops that used a folding glass rear window, cruise control, tilt-away steering wheel and wider styled steel wheels.

The 1967 Mustang was a better car, but competition from GM hurt sales. The Mustang still outsold all competitors combined, but the Mustang would no longer dominate the market in the same way it had.

Prospects

The 1967 Mustangs are less expensive to acquire but again convertible GTs lead the way in appreciation. K engine production hit a low, 472 units, so you are more likely to find Mustangs with the regular 289s or the 390. Get one with the 390 if you can. You'll also enjoy your Mustang more if you find one with air conditioning and the Interior Decor Group.

1967 Mustang GT equipment
200 hp 289 ci V-8; optional engines: 225 hp 289, 271 hp 289, 320 hp 390
3-speed manual transmission (4-speed manual mandatory with 271 hp 289 ci V-8)
Power front disc brakes
Grille-mounted foglamps
Heavy-duty suspension (heavy-duty springs and shocks, larger front sway bar)
Dual exhaust system with chrome quad extensions (with optional engines)
GT or GTA emblems
Lower body side stripes
GT pop-open gas cap
F70×14 Wide Oval WSW tires
Desirable options
4-speed manual or 3-speed automatic transmission
Styled steel wheels
Power steering
Air conditioning
Competition Handling Package (includes 15 inch wheels, $^{15}/_{16}$ inch front sway bar, Gabriel adjustable shocks)
Interior Decor Group
Center console
Fold-down rear seat (fastbacks)

Chapter 4

1968 Mustangs

★★	1968 Hardtop
★★★	1968 Fastback
★★★	1968 Convertible
★★★★	1968½ Cobra Jet
★★★★	1968 California Special
Add ★	1968 GT with 390 V-8
Add ★	With 427 engine

The 1968 Mustang received minor grille and trim modifications to set it off from the 1967. It also received some minor mechanical changes in order to comply with government safety rules. The most significant of these was a collapsible steering column. The most obvious visual changes were the deletion of the horizontal grille bars and of the

The 1968 Mustang GT fastback was basically a carryover.

37

View from the rear was unchanged as well.

simulated side scoops, and the use of side marker lights in the front and back.

Ford gave the interior a new steering wheel design and different upholstery patterns, and for the first time the rearview mirror was affixed directly on the windshield. The Interior Decor Group was distinguished by the use of woodgrain appliques on the dash and doors and by the use of a woodgrain steering wheel. More and more options were grouped together. The Sports Trim Group consisted of the woodgrain dash, knitted vinyl bucket seat inserts on hardtops and fastbacks, wheelwell moldings, two-toned louvered hood and Argent styled steel wheels with E70×14 Wide Oval whitewalls for V-8 Mustangs. The two-toned hood, which was available separately as well, tended to give a plain-Jane Mustang a performance look. The Protection Group of options included color-keyed rubber floor mats, door edge guards and chrome license plate frames. For use with the GT Group, the Reflective Group included reflective GT stripes and paint on the styled wheels.

The GT Equipment Group changed, the most prominent change being the addition of a C-stripe that followed the bodyside contour. This was an adaptation of the stripe that Ford had used on its long-distance racing Ford GT40s. However, side stripes like those offered in 1967 could be substituted. The familiar foglights remained, but the light bar between them was deleted. The lights were mounted directly on the grille. GT emblems on each front fender, GT pop-open gas cap and GT letters on the hubcaps identified the package visually.

Heavy-duty suspension components remained unchanged from 1967. Power front disc brakes became optional, but were mandatory when the larger 390 or 427 was ordered. The dual exhaust system with its chrome quad tips was standard on all GT engines (however, only 4V four-barrel car-

Grille bars were eliminated, and on the GTs, the foglamps were mounted directly on the grille.

The most noticeable change in the interior was the redesigned steering wheel and dash.

GTs came with this C-stripe on the side. All 1968 Mustangs came with front and rear side marker lights. The owner painted the wheels. *Perry Rivers*

buretor engines were available with the GT package), as were F70×14 WSW Firestone Wide Oval tires on six-inch-wide steel rims. The 14×6 inch styled steel wheels that were part of the GT Equipment Group either were painted Argent (a dull silver) or were chrome plated, and both used chrome trim rings and hubcaps with large GT letters. The 390 and 427 engines also came with chrome engine components (chrome valve covers, air cleaner lid and oil filler cap).

Engine selection was a bit more complicated than before. The standard engine was the 200 ci six-cylinder. Although both four-barrel 289s were deleted, the two-barrel version, now rated at 195 hp, continued until it was replaced by a two-barrel 302 by midyear. The highest rated small-block was now a 302, basically a stroked 289, rated at 230 hp. It used a hydraulic cam and a smallish 470 cfm Autolite four-barrel carburetor. Interestingly, the four-barrel 302 lasted only one year, and if you wanted to buy a Mustang with a four-barrel 302 (excluding the Boss 302), you had to wait until 1983.

The big 390 continued unchanged; however it was now rated at 325 hp. The largest engine available was a hydraulic cam 427 rated at 390 hp at 5600 rpm. The 427, however, was only available for a short time dur-

GTs had new styled steel wheels, with either Argent (dull silver) or chrome centers.

Rear seat room was barely adequate.

Still, the 427 was Ford's best engine, and it had a tremendous race heritage. A member of the FE series, the 427 was first introduced in 1963, and it became an engine of many variations.

For the 1968 Mustang, a Low Riser version was installed using a low-rise intake manifold. This particular version used cylinder heads similiar to production 390 heads, but with slightly larger valves.

The biggest difference between the 427 and other FE series engines was the cylinder block. The 427 block was superior for two reasons. It had stronger cross-bolt main caps and a much better oiling system, which incorporated an oil passage at the side of the block. For this reason, the 427 is sometimes referred to as the Sideoiler.

The 427 wasn't popular because of its limited production run and cost. Some sources have criticized it for lack of performance. If you look at the 427 closely, you'll see that it was not too different from the 428 Cobra Jet (428CJ) that replaced it. The 427 used the same camshaft (but with a different part number), and the 427's cylinder heads actually had slightly smaller intake ports than those on the 428. The 427 did have a larger bore-to-stroke ratio, which meant it produced power at a higher rpm. The 428CJ, on the other hand, has been criticized for producing too much low-end torque. Other

ing the 1968 model run, and it was phased out in December 1967.

Although the 427 was Ford's premier race engine, it had some disadvantages as installed in the Mustang. It was available only with an automatic transmission, and it could have used a larger carburetor than the stock 650 cfm Holley to take advantage of the engine's true potential. More important, its cost of $622 put the engine out of reach of most enthusiasts.

The fold-down rear seat continued to be a popular option on the fastbacks.

By mid-year, the 302 had replaced the 289 as the smallest V-8 available. This is the 230 hp four-barrel version.

1968 Mustang GT equipment
230 hp 302 ci V-8; optional engines: 325 hp 390 and 390 hp 427
3-speed manual transmission (3-speed automatic mandatory with 427)
Grille-mounted foglamps
Heavy-duty suspension (stiffer springs and shocks, larger front sway bar)
Dual exhaust system with chrome quad extensions
GT emblems on front fenders
GT pop-open gas cap
GT side C-stripes
F70×14 Wide Oval WSW tires
Chrome engine components (390 and 427 engines)
Power front disc brakes (mandatory, extra cost with 390 and 427)
GT styled steel wheels with chrome trim rings and GT hubcap
Desirable options
4-speed manual or 3-speed automatic transmission
Power steering
Power brakes
Air conditioning
Fold-down rear seat (fastbacks)
Limited-slip differential
Center console
Interior Decor Group

Besides the rare 427, the largest engine option was still the 390, rated at 325 hp for 1968. Note the owner-installed air cleaner.

than the smaller carburetor and limitation of an automatic transmission, performance of the two engines was basically the same. The 427 just cost too much.

The mid-year introduction was the 1968½ Cobra Jet. They were all GTs with the addition of a black hood stripe and hood scoop. *George Wahl*

41

The Cobra Jet hood scoop was functional. *George Wahl*

Specials
Cobra Jet

To counter criticism that the Mustang couldn't hold its own against more powerful competitors, Ford, on April 1, 1968, introduced the 428 Cobra Jet engine as an option on fastback and hardtop Mustangs; these were the Cobra Jet Mustangs. The engine, more reasonable in cost, offered excellent street performance and thus was attractive to the enthusiast.

A Cobra Jet Mustang was more than just an engine option. The lower front suspension shock towers were strengthened. A functional Ram Air induction setup and revised rear suspension shock absorber mounting for four-speed cars were included. By staggering the shocks, one in front of the axle and the other behind it, wheel hop during hard acceleration was largely eliminated. This was not a Ford exclusive; the Camaro also had staggered shocks in 1968. The Ram Air induction system was also good for a 0.2 second improvement in quarter-mile times.

The 428CJ was available with either a four-speed manual or a C-6 automatic. Standard axle ratio was 3.50:1, while 3.91:1

The big 428CJ had a unique flapper valve air cleaner. *George Wahl*

or 4.30:1 ratios were optional for even more acceleration. On this Mustang, a black hood stripe covered the hood scoop and cowl, and the GT Equipment Group was mandatory.

The 428CJ engine was basically a production 428 fitted with 427 Low Riser cylinder heads. The heads, however, used intake ports that were slightly larger, similar in size to those found on the Medium Riser 427. The camshaft was identical to the one in the Low Riser and 390 GT engines, but a larger 735 cfm Holley carburetor was mounted on a cast-iron copy of the 428 Police Interceptor intake manifold. The 428CJ also used an oil pan windage tray. It was rated at 335 hp at 5200 rpm, which was obviously on the low side.

Instead of the Firestone Wide Ovals, the 428CJ Mustangs got Goodyear Polyglas F70×14 tires mounted on the GT styled steel wheels. These were the best street tires available at the time and made their debut on this Mustang. The 428CJ Mustangs also came with thirty-one-spline rear axles.

According to drag racing magazines, the 428CJ was able to crank out quarter-mile times in the low- to mid-thirteen-second range; other magazines recorded times in the low- to mid-fourteens. Obviously appealing to drag-oriented customers, cars supplied to hot rod magazines for testing were specially tuned by Ford, a common practice at the time. So-called test cars usually were delivered on company trailers for testing, with several engineers to ensure that they functioned properly.

A total of 2,253 fastbacks and 564 hardtops with the 428CJ were built, all collector

Cobra Jet Mustangs were built as hardtops as well. *Rex Hall*

items now. Few, however, have survived. An unknown number of convertibles were built as well.

Regional specials

Several specialty Mustangs were sold during 1968. There was the Mustang Sprint, a special option package available on both six-cylinder and V-8 Mustangs. On the sixes, the package included GT side stripes, a pop-open gas cap and full wheel covers. The V-8s got in addition the Wide Oval tires on styled steel wheels and the GT foglamps.

More significant was the California Special. Available mostly in California, the GT/CS was a trim package for the hardtop Mustang which used many GT and Shelby Mustang styling features. The most obvious was the Shelby rear deck lid with integral spoiler and sequential taillights. Shelby side scoops were also used, but these were non-functional. A blacked-out front grille without any Mustang emblems used rectangular Lucas or Marchal foglamps. The GT/CS also got a distinctive side stripe that began at the front fender and terminated at the side scoop. Wheels were the styled steel wheels without the GT identification. The GT/CS could be had with any regular production Mustang engine. Production estimates are in the 5,000 range.

Similar to the GT/CS was the High Country Special, another limited edition Mus-

---

1968½ Cobra Jet Mustang
428 Cobra Jet Ram Air engine
GT Equipment Group*
Power disc brakes*
8000 rpm tachometer in dash on all 4-speed cars, optional on automatics*
Lower shock tower bracing
Ram Air induction (functional hood scoop with no turn signal indicators)
Staggered rear shock absorbers on all 4-speed cars
Gloss-black stripe on hood*
F70×14 Goodyear Polyglas RWL belted tires
* *Does not apply to initial cars with body numbers in the 135,000 range*

The California Special is the best-known of the many Special Mustangs that were built. *Clay Holland*

tang, this time sold by Colorado dealers. It was identical to the GT/CS, except that the California Special identification was deleted and the GT/CS on the side scoop was replaced by a High Country Special decal. High Country Specials had been available in Colorado since 1966, but the only thing "special" about them were the two badges located on the front fenders. Other Specials offered in 1968 included the Sunshine Special and the Nebraska Big Red.

With all the different specials and option groups, it was becoming evident that Ford was widening the Mustang's appeal and marketing it to specific niches. We would see more of this strategy during 1969-70.

1968 GT/CS California Special equipment
Shelby fiberglass rear deck lid and fiberglass extensions
Sequential taillights
Nonfunctional side scoops
GT/CS side and rear deck stripes
California Special rear fender emblems
Blacked-out grille with Marchal or Lucas foglamps
Styled steel wheels and pop-open gas cap without GT emblems
Click-type hood locks

Prospects

The 1968½ CJ is the most sought after 1968 Mustang followed by the GTs. The 427 Mustangs are extremely rare too. These are seldom seen or advertised, which leads one to believe that few survived. If you can't find one of these, the GT convertibles and fastbacks with the 390 engine are good alternatives.

There isn't much difference between the 1967 and 1968 Mustangs in terms of prices. It is really a matter of taste. Those favoring the 1967 probably notice that the 1967s have many visual features that are common to the 1965-66 Mustangs, such as the optional wheels, GT stripes and the small-block engines. The 1968 Mustangs have features that are found on the 1969s: styled steel wheels, more blatant striping and blacked-out hoods—and more emphasis on performance.

Rust is still the major problem with 1967-68 Mustangs. Again, unless you are looking at a big-engined convertible GT, you are still better off not restoring a badly rusted-out car. As performance became a more dominant theme, you can be sure that 427/428 Mustangs were abused at some point and probably modified as well. Look at these cars closely.

Chapter 5

1969 Mustangs

★★	1969 Hardtop
★★★	1969 Fastback
★★★	1969 Convertible
★★★	1969 Mach 1
★★★★	1969 Boss 302
★★★★★	1969 Boss 429
Add ★	With 428CJ/CJ-R

The year 1969 was an important one for the Mustang. It was significantly restyled, yet you could easily trace its origin because the car retained all the Mustang styling cues. It was lower, sleeker and meaner, and while the car grew in size, it still used a 108 inch wheelbase. The restyle was particularly effective on the fastback, now called the SportsRoof, and all performance Mustangs were based on it. In fact, over forty-four percent of all Mustangs sold that year were fastbacks.

Most interior and exterior dimensions grew in 1969, although not drastically. More importantly, all Mustangs were lowered 0.5 inch on the suspension, and the windshield

The 1969 styling was best exemplified by the sleek fastback. This particular Mach 1 has a rare non-Ram Air 428CJ. *Bob Stanworth*

GT Mustangs were still available in all three body styles. An obvious change from previous GTs was the deletion of the foglamps.

rake was increased by 2.2 degrees. This translated to about a 150–175 pound weight increase depending on the model.

In comparison to the Mach 1, the GTs looked almost plain.

The roofline on the SportsRoof was lowered by 0.9 inch. The side sculpturing was eliminated for a cleaner, smoother look, but the biggest visual changes were the front grille and the rear tail treatment on the SportsRoof. The revised front grille was enlarged and used four four-inch headlights for a decidedly aggressive look. The Sports-Roof also received simulated side scoops and a spoilered rear, similar to the Shelby Mustang's but less pronounced.

The restyled interior was rather effective in carrying the racer theme inside, particularly on cars that came with the Deluxe Interior Decor Group (the Mach 1, Boss 429 and Grande): it used simulated woodgrain appliques on the instrument panel, doors and console. Cars with this interior also got a round clock on the passenger side of the dash panel; it looked nice, but it was difficult for the driver to read. The Deluxe Interior Decor Group was optional only on the SportsRoof and convertibles.

Speaking of interiors, there was also the Interior Decor Group, which used Comfortweave upholstery on the seats, molded door panels with wood applique, deluxe three-spoke Rim-Blow steering wheel and a remote rectangular mirror on the driver's side. High-back bucket seats, first seen on 1969 Mustangs, were available with either interior option.

If you ordered a tachometer, you also got a different arrangement of the dash pods for the driver's side. The tachometer took the place of the standard fuel and temperature gauges on the large right side pod. The temperature gauge was then relocated to the far left small pod (which displaced the standard alternator gauge), and the necessary fuel gauge took the place of the standard oil pressure gauge on the far right small pod. It would have been nice if Ford could have retained the alternator and oil pressure gauges as it had done with the Shelby interior.

The option list included some new items for 1969. The Exterior Decor Group consisted of rocker panel moldings, wheelwell and rear end moldings as well as the base five-spoke full wheel cover. Additional interior lights were an option. Intermittent windshield wipers, power ventilation and radial tires were all new 1969 options.

The standard engine was still the 200 ci six-cylinder with a three-speed manual transmission. The three-speed manual was standard equipment on all engines up to the 351 four-barrel. The three-speed Cruise-O-Matic was optional on all engines. A larger six-cylinder measuring 250 ci was also available. With this engine, you could get air conditioning if you desired, whereas you could not with the 200 ci version.

The smallest optional V-8 was a two-barrel version of the 302 rated at 210 hp. Next in line were two versions of a new engine: the 351W, basically a stretched 302.

By increasing the stroke of the 302 to 3.5 inches, the block's height was raised by one inch to accommodate the longer stroke. At the same time, the crank journals were resized, resulting in an engine that had no interchangeability with the 289/302 engines, save for the heads. The heads, by the way, did have slightly larger ports. Because the engine was built at Ford's Windsor plant, it came to be known as the 351W. Ford's other 351, the 351C built in Cleveland, was available on Mustangs from 1970 through 1973. The 351W was the only 351 ci V-8 that was available on 1969 Mustangs. The 351W was rated at 250 hp with a 350 cfm two-barrel Autolite carburetor and 290 hp with a

Rare are the GT convertibles. This one was equipped with a 390. *Van Reed*

Also rare are the 428CJ GTs. I spotted this hardtop in Paris, France.

47

This rare 428CJ fastback GT resides in Long Island, New York.

All GTs came with the regular Mustang interior as standard equipment. This one also has the optional console.

Much more attractive was the optional Deluxe Interior Group, which was standard equipment on the Mach 1, Grande and Boss 429. Shifter is non-stock.

The Mach 1 looked fast just sitting still. On this example the owner installed the front spoiler, rear wing and Sports Slats. *Kevin Zehr*

There were several Mach 1 styling features. The simulated side scoops were created with the Mach 1 in mind, but came on all fastbacks.

470 cfm four-barrel. It was a good design with a strong bottom end; however, restrictive porting and valves for an engine this size limit performance to low- to mid-range rpm. In stock or modified form, a comparably modified 351C will run circles around the 351W.

The old 390 was still available to bridge the gap between the 351s and the 428s.

Also standard equipment on the Mach 1 was this simulated hood scoop. Plate on each side indicated engine displacement.

Rated at 320 hp, its Holley carburetor was replaced by a 470 cfm Autolite unit. Acceleration over the 351 4V was negligible while tending to detract from the car's handling. The 390 really wasn't much of a performance engine.

> **1969 Mustang GT equipment**
> 250 hp 351W V-8; optional engines: 290 hp 351W, 320 hp 390, 335 hp 428CJ
> Competition Suspension (heavy-duty springs and shocks, larger front sway bar)
> Lower body side stripes
> Dual exhaust system with chrome quad extensions (with optional engines)
> Argent-painted styled steel wheels with chrome trim rings and GT hubcaps
> E70X14 WSW belted tires
> Pin-type hood lock latches
> Nonfunctional hood scoop with integral turn signal indication lights; Shaker scoop standard with 428CJ Ram Air engine
> 3-speed manual transmission
> 4-wheel drum brakes
> **Desirable options**
> Power steering and power front disc brakes
> 4-speed manual or 3-speed automatic transmission
> Deluxe interior
> Air conditioning
> Chrome styled steel wheels with chrome trim rings and GT hubcaps

Specials

The same 428 Cobra Jet engine introduced in 1968½ Cobra Jet Mustang was the top engine option; however it was available in three versions. The first 428CJ was available without a functional hood scoop. An additional $133 got you the second version known as the 428 Cobra Jet Ram Air, which had the unique Shaker hood scoop. The scoop incorporated a trap door that let outside cool air enter the air cleaner whenever the gas pedal was floored. It worked, too, as quarter-mile times usually improved by 2 mph and 0.2 seconds. The Shaker scoop, connected directly on the engine, moved along with any engine movement which really gave a Mustang equipped with this engine the edge in 1969.

The third version was known as the 428 Super Cobra Jet Ram Air (428SCJ). It came with the Shaker scoop but had some additional important features. The 428SCJ was

Blacked-out hood also used NASCAR-type hood pins for a racer image. This 390 powered Mach 1 has the optional Shaker scoop, which was optional on the 351 and larger V-8s.

available only when a 3.91:1 or 4.30:1 axle ratio was ordered, and it differed mainly from the other versions because the engine had special cap screw connecting rods, similar to the 427 Le Mans rods. These were much stronger and accordingly, gave more reliable higher engine rpm. Part of the SCJ package included an engine oil cooler, mounted in front of the radiator. This was good for a thirty-degree drop in engine oil temperature, again a measure to increase reliability. Ford did not issue a different engine code for the SCJ, but any 428CJ-R Mustangs with the axle code V for 3.91:1 or W for 4.30:1 were SCJs.

Besides the standard Mustangs, 1969 saw the addition of two special Mustangs designed to appeal to a particular segment of the market. The first of these was the Mustang Grande. The Grande was a luxury version of the Mustang hardtop designed to compete with Mercury's Cougar and the luxury versions of the Camaro and the Firebird.

Standard on the Mach 1 were these chrome styled steel wheels.

The smallest 4V engine on the GTs and Mach 1 was the 290 hp 351.

The biggest engine available in 1969 was the 428CJ. This non-Ram Air version came with chrome-plated valve covers. *Bob Stanworth*

On the outside, the Grande got wire wheel covers, dual color-keyed mirrors, a two-tone paint stripe, wheelwell rocker panel and rear deck moldings and Grande script lettering on each C-pillar.

The interior was the Deluxe Decor Group plus a special insulation package that added fifty-five pounds to the Mustang's weight. This insulation consisted of thick, heavy sound-deadening pads underneath the carpets. Any engine was available with the Grande.

During the year, another special Mustang, called the Mustang E, was introduced for the miserly segment of the market. The E came with the 250 ci six-cylinder coupled to an automatic transmission with a high-stall torque converter, and it used a low

The Ram Air 428CJ with Shaker scoop came with finned aluminum valve covers, as did all late 1969 non-Ram Air versions.

numerical axle ratio, 2.33:1. Rarely seen, the Mustang E was available only on the Sports-Roof Mustang body.

Mach 1

More significant was the new Mach 1, which took the place of the GT as the premier performance Mustang. Stripes, scoops and spoilers accentuated the image of a racer for the street which promised incredible performance. The hood was painted flat black with body color trim, and had a simulated hood scoop similar to the one on the 1968½ Cobra Jet Mustang. NASCAR-style hood-pin latches (an option) enhanced the race car image; reflective side and tail stripes coordinated with the body color; a chrome pop-open gas cap and chrome styled steel wheels added to the package. The four-barrel carburetor engines got the usual chrome quad-tipped dual exhaust system. The handling suspension, now called the Competition Suspension, consisted of heavier springs and shocks, a larger diameter front sway bar and staggered rear shocks for four-speed Mach

If your Mach 1 is original and has this engine oil cooler in front of the radiator, then it has the 428SCJ-R engine. The oil cooler was also standard equipment on Boss 429 Mustangs.

All 428CJ powered Mustangs came with additional shock tower bracing. This is what the standard shock tower looks like.

The bracing consisted of additional material welded on the tower to resist flexing. This particular Mustang has the upper control arm mounts lowered for better handling.

1s to control rear wheel hop. Standard tires were E70×14 WSW belted tires, while F70×14 Goodyear Polyglas GTs with raised letters were mandatory on the 428 ci Mach 1s. Incidentally, the radial tire option was not available with the 428 Cobra Jet.

The Mach 1 also had some industry firsts. The body-colored racing mirrors, standard on the Mach 1, have since been widely copied, as has the Shaker hood scoop that came with the 428CJ Ram Air engine. In 1970, the Firebird Trans Am got a Shaker-type scoop as did Chrysler's Barracuda and Challenger. The Shaker was also optional on the 351 and 390s.

Ford also gave the Mach 1 a particularly nice feature, the Deluxe Interior Group: Rim-Blow steering wheel, console, special high-back bucket seats and fifty-five pound insulation package. Because previous GT Mustangs did not have this fine interior as standard equipment, many earlier performance Mustangs ended up with the base interior, which tended to detract from the total GT concept.

Standard engine for the Mach 1 was the 351 two-barrel V-8, with the other V-8s optional. As you can expect, the 428CJ Ram Air engine was the one to get, and today it is the most desirable in a 1969 Mach 1.

Performance with the big 428 was similar to that of the 1968½ Cobra Jet Mustang,

---

1969 Mach 1 Mustang
SportsRoof body
250 hp 351W V-8; optional engines: 290 hp 351W, 320 hp 390, 335 hp 428CJ
3-speed manual transmission
Competition Suspension (heavier springs and shocks and larger front sway bar)
Deluxe interior with center console. Rim-Blow deluxe steering wheel, electric clock, high-back bucket seats
Color-keyed dual racing mirrors
Blacked-out hood and cowl
Nonfunctional hood scoop
Hood latches with cable-connected click pins
Reflective side and rear deck stripes
Rocker panel molding
Dual exhaust system with chrome quad extensions (optional engines only)
Pop-open gas cap
E70×14 WSW tires on chrome styled steel wheels (F70×14 RWL with 428CJ engine)
Desirable options
4-speed manual or 3-speed automatic transmission
Power steering
Power front disc brakes
428CJ Ram Air engine with Shaker hood scoop
Traction Lok differential
Drag Pack (includes 428SCJ-Ram Air engine, Shaker scoop, 3.91:1 or 4.30:1 axle ratio, engine oil cooler)
Fold-down rear seat
Air conditioning

On this 1969 Boss 302 Mustang, note the deleted side scoop. *Randy Ream*

with quarter-mile times reported in the high-thirteen- to low-fourteen-second range. Considering tire technology in the late sixties, these were excellent times, especially since the 428CJ was known for its tremendous low-end torque. The F70×14 tires were just not enough tire. The big-block Mach 1s would have been better off with the wider F60×15 Goodyears, which were standard equipment on the Bosses and came with most 1969 Shelby Mustangs.

The Mach 1 has been called the supercar of the masses, and production was high. How could you resist the styling? Ford built 72,450 Mach 1s in 1969, and while 13,193 of the 1969 Mustangs came with a version of the 428CJ, quite likely ninety-five percent of these were Mach 1s. As prices for Shelby and Boss Mustangs have been rising strongly in the past few years, the 428 Mach 1 is starting to become a viable alternative.

Not to be forgotten was the Mustang GT, which was still available in 1969, catering to those who were put off by the Mach 1's flash. Engine availability was identical to that of the Mach 1. The GT Equipment

Liberal use of low gloss black paint helped to transform the Mustang fastback into the Boss 302. The hood got the same paint treatment as the Mach 1, but did not get the NASCAR hood pins. *Randy Ream*

Black paint was also applied on each outside headlight bucket on the Boss 302. *Randy Ream*

Group followed tradition to the end and was still available on all three Mustang body styles. The option consisted of rocker panel stripes, GT gas cap, styled steel wheels with GT identification, NASCAR-style hood-pin latches, dual exhausts with chrome quad outlets (on four-barrel engines) and heavy-duty suspension.

Only 4,973 GTs were sold. But it is possible to come up with some interesting combinations, such as a GT convertible with a 428 CJ Ram Air and the deluxe interior.

A point to remember is that standard brakes on all 1969 Mustangs were drums, even on the Mach 1. If you are interested in one of the more powerful Mustangs, you should try to get a car that has the power front disc brake option, simply for safety's sake. Power steering is good, too.

Boss 302

In 1969, Ford also introduced two really special Mustangs, the Boss 302 and the Boss 429.

Two reasons motivated Ford's decision to build the Boss 302 Mustang. First, enthusiasts in-the-know wanted a balanced car that could provide not only good acceleration but good handling and braking as well. The only such car on the market in 1968 was the Camaro Z-28, which sold 7,199 units, and for which predictions of 1969 sales hit 20,000 units. The Z-28 also won ten out of the thirteen races in the Trans-Am series.

Ford was heavily involved in the Sports Car Club of America (SCCA) Trans-Am series in which pony cars raced with factory support. Although Ford won the series in 1966 and 1967, Chevrolet trounced the Mustang in 1968. Ford developed the Boss 302 engine to replace the unreliable Tunnel-Port 302. For the Ford teams to be able to use the engine, SCCA rules required that at least 1,000 cars with this engine be sold to the public. The Boss 302 Mustang was born. Ford originally wanted to call this the Mustang Trans Am but since Pontiac had rights

The rear deck and taillight panel were also painted black on the Boss 302. Unique rear spoiler was optional. *Randy Ream*

All Boss 302s came with 15×7 inch Magnum 500 wheels, painted argent. The chrome versions were optional. *Randy Ream*

The stock Boss 302 engine came with chrome steel valve covers and chrome air cleaner lid.

The big Holley 780 four-barrel sat on an aluminum high rise intake manifold on the Boss 302. *Randy Ream*

57

to that name, Ford decided to call the new Mustang a Boss 302 as well.

The Boss 302 was based on the 1969 SportsRoof body, but without the simulated sidebody scoops. Ford wanted to produce a car that purists could appreciate, so anything that wasn't functional was eliminated. Visually, the Boss 302 was daring; it had a purposeful, racy look. The hood was blacked-out, as was the area around the outside headlights, the rear deck area and the rear taillight panel. A large C-stripe with Boss 302 lettering decorated the sides. Exterior color choice was limited to just four colors: Wimbledon White, Bright Yellow, Calypso Coral and Acapulco Blue.

The Boss 302 also used a front spoiler designed to keep the nose of the car down at high speeds. Popular Boss 302 options were the rear wing and the rear window slats. The adjustable wing was designed to control the rear at high speeds, while the slats just enhanced the appearance of the car. Although roof slats originally were seen in a Corvair prototype in 1963 and on the Lamborghini Miura, it was the Boss 302 that popularized roof slats.

Part of the Boss 302's visual impact turned on the standard Argent-painted Magnum 500 wheels (chrome was optional) mounting the large F60×15 Goodyear Polyglas tires. These were the best street tires available at the time. With these tires, the Boss 302 was able to generate high cornering speeds, which unfortunately resulted in failure of front-suspension control-arm mounting points on Boss 302 prototypes. For this reason, all Boss 302s have reinforced shock towers, along with larger spindles to handle the extra cornering loads.

Unlike other performance Mustangs, the Boss 302 was a complete package with a

While the standard Boss 302 interior was regular Mustang, this one has the optional console and high-back bucket seats. *Randy Ream*

The limited-production 1969 Boss 429 looked almost plain against the decked out Mach 1 and Boss 302. Even though the 429 looked understated, its lower stance, front spoiler and large hood scoop meant high performance.

Although the Sports Slats and rear deck spoiler weren't part of the Boss 429, many owners have installed them.

59

limited number of options. The only engine available was the Boss 302, mated to a wide-ratio four-speed manual. A 3.50:1 rear axle ratio was standard, with 3.91:1 and 4.30:1 optional. Additional standard features were front disc brakes, quick-ratio steering (16:1) with power assist recommended, staggered rear shocks and color-keyed rearview mirrors. The fenders were radiused to clear the wide F60 tires and also identify a Boss 302. Most Boss 302s came with the standard Mustang interior, although the deluxe interior was optional.

Of course, what made the Boss 302 different was the engine. The block was a strengthened version of the production 302 block, with four-bolt main caps. It used a forged-steel crankshaft with forged connecting rods that were the same as those found on the old High Performance 289. All this was done to ensure reliability.

The reason for the excellent power output was the redesigned cylinder heads. These had extremely large intake and exhaust ports, canted valves measuring 2.23 inches on the intake and 1.72 inches on the exhaust and adjustable rocker arms. In comparison, the High Performance 289 had valves measuring 1.78 inches intake and 1.44 inches exhaust. An aluminum high-rise intake manifold with a large Holley 780 cfm Holley four-barrel provided induction on the Boss. A subdued mechanical lifter camshaft was used as was a dual-point distributor and dual

All Boss 429s were built at Kar Kraft, Ford's Special Vehicle Division. *Ford Motor Company*

1969 Boss 302 Mustang
SportsRoof body without simulated side scoops
Color-keyed dual racing mirrors
Front spoiler
Low-gloss black paint on outside headlight area, hood, cowl, rear deck lid, taillight panel
Boss 302 side stripes
Argent-painted Magnum 500 15×7 inch wheels with F60×15 Goodyear Polyglas GT tires
290 hp Boss 302 engine with chrome valve covers, aluminum intake manifold, Holley 780 cfm carburetor, electronic rev-limiter, dual exhaust system
4-speed manual transmission
Quick-ratio steering
Power front disc brakes
3.50:1 rear axle ratio
Staggered rear shock absorbers

Desirable options
Rear deck spoiler
Rear window slats
High-back bucket seats
Deluxe interior with console
Chrome Magnum 500 15×7 inch wheels
8000 rpm tachometer
Power steering
Traction Lok differential

exhaust system. Very little else was really necessary to convert the Boss 302 into a full-blown race engine.

To ensure reliability on the street, Ford installed a rev-limiter, which stopped the engine from revving over 6150 rpm. The engine was good to 7000 rpm, with an occasional burst to 7500 rpm. Even with the rev-limiter, the Boss 302 was rated at 290 hp at 5800 rpm.

Obviously underrated, the Boss 302 could cover the quarter-mile in the high-fourteen-second range and make 0–60 mph times under seven seconds.

The Boss 302 was enthusiastically received; finally a Mustang that could handle with the best and had supercar acceleration to boot. It provided Ford with a base for a better Trans-Am racer, and although it came in second in the 1969, the Boss 302 took the 1970 series.

The only thing to watch out for in a Boss 302 are the stock pistons, which usually cracked after between 10,000 and 30,000 miles; a rebuild was then needed. If you find an original Boss 302 with under 30,000 miles, plan to rebuild the engine, unless of course you trailer the car.

All Boss 429s came with this KK (for Kar Kraft) tape strip in addition to the regular warranty plate. Boss 429s, Boss 302s and Shelby Mustangs came with plates that read "Special Performance Vehicle."

You can expect these beauties to appreciate, although they still don't quite have the stature of a Shelby Mustang. The Boss 302 is a true thoroughbred, but it just doesn't have the magic of the Shelby name.

Boss 429

Many consider the Boss 429 to be the ultimate Mustang, and I must admit that I am partial to them, as I have owned two of

Trunk mounted battery, standard on the Boss 429, improved weight distribution.

61

Standard wheels on the 1969 Boss 429s were chrome 15×7 Magnum 500s with long center hubcaps.

these beasts. Through most of the seventies, the Boss 429 was hardly known, with most attention fixed on the rapidly appreciating Shelby Mustangs, and to a lesser extent, the Boss 302. Even when it was available for sale, the Boss 429 was pretty low-key, rarely seen and not promoted. Today, of course, the situation has changed dramatically.

In many ways, the Boss 429 was similar to the early 1965-66 Shelby Mustangs. They were both built on a special production line, and both received many expensive, unique hand-built modifications. It was more than just a case of dropping a big (really big) engine in the Mustang chassis.

The Boss 429 Mustang came into being to satisfy NASCAR rules—the sanctioning body that regulated stock car racing, a most important area in Ford's racing program in the 1960s. To stay competitive with Chrysler's 426 Hemi, Ford developed its own version of the Hemi engine, but with some innovations. NASCAR rules stated that if Ford wanted to race this engine, at least 500 cars with the engine had to be built and sold to the general public. It would have seemed more logical to install this new engine in the Torino but it was decided on the Mustang instead.

The standard 375 hp Boss 429 engine.

Ford instituted a crash program to develop and build the necessary 500 cars. The Boss 429 was no ordinary engine. Being physically large, the engine necessitated the enlarging and modifying of the Mustang's engine compartment. Ford subcontracted this to Kar Kraft, which also built many of Ford's race and experimental cars.

Ford shipped 1969 SportsRoof Mustangs that normally would have received the 428SCJ engine to Kar Kraft. There, the spring towers were moved outward and reinforced. At the same time, the suspension mounting points were relocated by lowering and moving them outward by one inch, much in the way the suspension of the all-out race Boss 302 Mustang was modified. Then the complete engine and transmission combination was lowered as a unit into the car.

Externally, the Boss 429 retained the simulated side scoops of the SportsRoof Mustang and also used the color-keyed side view mirrors. Like the Boss 302, the Boss 429 used a front spoiler, although it was slightly shallower as the car sat lower. The only other visual clues were the fender decals and the large hood scoop. Wheels were chrome Magnum 500s, using the Goodyear F60×15 tires. Because the Boss 429 preceded the

Quite a few Boss 429 owners have modified their engines.

This Boss 429 has a Ford race intake featuring two four-barrel carburetors, adapted for street use.

Boss 302 by about two months, the Boss 429 has the distinction of being the first Mustang and first car to have these tires. Only one interior was available: the deluxe interior with console, 8000 rpm tachometer, Rim-Blow steering wheel and fifty-five pounds of sound-deadening insulation.

Standard Boss 429 features included engine oil cooler, trunk-mounted battery, power disc brakes, power steering, close-ratio four-speed manual transmission, staggered rear shocks, manual choke and manually operated hood scoop. Although the 4.30:1 Detroit Locker rear was optional, most cars came with the 3.91:1 Traction Lok rear. The Boss 429 had the heaviest springs ever installed in a production Mustang and a $^{15}/_{16}$ inch front sway bar—and it was the first to have a rear sway bar, in this case measuring ¾ inch. The dual exhaust system, identical to the 428CJ system, did not have the chrome exhaust tips, and most Boss 429s came with the plain gas cap.

Boss 429s were available in six colors: Raven Black, Black Jade, Royal Maroon, Candy Apple Red, Wimbledon White and Blue.

The 429 engine was labeled 429CJ-R HO on the driver's door, but it has also been called the Blue Crescent 429, the Shotgun 429, Twisted Hemi 429 and, of course, the Boss 429. Although the Mustang received many specialized parts, it is the engine that made this Mustang unique. In simple terms, aluminum cylinder heads were mated to the cast-iron 429 engine block; on closer examination how the Boss 429 differed from other engines was clear.

The cylinder block, while similar in appearance to other 429/460 blocks, was cast from nodular iron and was much harder. It also has a unique four-gallery oiling system, four-bolt main caps and thick cylinder walls that could be overbored by 0.160 inch. The crankshaft was forged steel, as were the rods, and the engine used 10.5:1 compres-

The Ram Box intake was another Ford race intake manifold adapted for street use on this particular Boss 429.

sion pistons. Such a strong bottom end was necessary to cope with the extra power the aluminum cylinder heads produced. They featured modified (crescent) hemispherical combustion chambers, extremely large intake and exhaust ports and valves among the largest of any production engine ever.

Intake valves measured 2.28 inches while exhausts were 1.90 inches, arranged in a crossflow position to enhance upper-rpm performance. The Hemi design was known for its strong mid- to upper-rpm performance; Ford tried to combine the strong low-end performance of the wedge combustion chamber design with the high-end of the Hemi. Another interesting feature was the dry-deck method of mounting the heads on the block; no conventional head gasket was used. Instead, copper O-rings sealed the cylinders while rubber Viton rings were used on the water and oil passages. A Holley 735 cfm carburetor, a mild hydraulic camshaft, an aluminum high-rise intake manifold, aluminum valve covers, free-flowing exhaust manifolds, a dual-point distributor and a six-quart oil pan were all part of the Boss 429 engine.

Ford installed two versions of this engine in the Boss 429 Mustang, known as the S and T engines. The S engines had much larger connecting rods, using ½ inch rod bolts (the rods weighed almost three pounds each!), similar to the ones used on the NASCAR 429s, while the more common T engine used slightly stronger production 429 rods. For once, Ford rated the engines accurately: 375 hp at 5200 rpm, as dynomometer tests showed that this was the actual power output of both versions of the street Boss 429 engine.

In spite of all these impressive specifications, the Boss 429 did not turn out to be the street terror it was expected to be. The small carburetor, mild camshaft and heavy valvetrain limited performance tremendously. Chrysler's 426 Hemi, on the other hand, was a real tiger, with two four-barrel carburetors and, until 1970, a pretty strong mechanical camshaft.

Still, the Boss 429 could keep up with the 428CJ Mustangs and from 60 mph on, would leave them behind. However, its handling was superior to that of any other big-block Mustang and better than most of the smaller-engined Mustangs as well. The revised front suspension geometry, wider track and rear sway bar combined to eliminate most of the understeer from the chassis. The Boss 429 was more precise, quicker and more responsive during cornering. It felt more like a detuned racer.

1969 Boss 429 Mustang
SportsRoof body
Color-keyed dual racing mirrors
Front spoiler
Boss 429 fender decals
Manually controlled hood scoop
Boss 429 375 hp V-8 with aluminum cylinder heads, intake manifold and valve covers
4-speed close-ratio manual transmission
Engine oil cooler
Trunk-mounted battery
Power steering
Power disc brakes
Special High Performance suspension with front and rear sway bars, staggered rear shock absorbers
Chrome 15×7 inch Magnum 500 wheels with F60×15 Goodyear Polyglas GT RWL tires, long-style center hubcaps
3.91:1 Traction Lok differential
Deluxe interior with clock and console
8000 rpm tachometer
AM radio

Prospects

You'll find that most Boss 429s are relatively low mileage cars. The engine is notorious for spinning bearings because the stock oil capacity is inadequate when the engine is revved over 6000 rpm. A lot of these cars were just parked early on after their owners found out that they weren't the killer street car they should have been (and most likely after spinning the bearings, too). The usual hotrod engine modifications, however, will transform this engine.

Production exceeded the NASCAR minimum of 500 with 899 units built, making the Boss 429 one of the rarest Mustangs. It is also one of the most difficult to fake.

Boss 429 Mustangs are quickly appreciating; soon they will be beyond the reach of most Mustang enthusiasts. Because they are so unique and use so many unique parts, they are more difficult to restore than other Mustangs. They are worth the challenge.

A point worth noting is that the Boss 302 and Boss 429 are the only Mustangs that have the car's consecutive unit number inscribed on the engine. On the Boss 302, this is at the top rear of the block, while on the Boss 429 it is at the rear and side. Obviously, a Boss 429 or 302 with the original engine is more valuable.

The years 1969 and 1970 were the high point for performance Mustangs. Mach 1s are starting to come out of the woodwork and are popular. Naturally, the 428 Mach 1s are leading the way in terms of appreciation as Ford built fewer. These offer tremendous acceleration in an exciting visual package.

Prices for Boss 302s and 429s have peaked. Parts availability, for both cars is limited—particularly the unique Boss 429 pieces.

Parts availability, for the 1969–70 cars, in general, is somewhat less than what is available for 1965–68 Mustangs, at least from the reproduction point of view. But as demand increases, you can be sure that someone will fill the gap.

Chapter 6

1970 Mustangs

★★	1970 Hardtop
★★★	1970 Fastback
★★★	1970 Convertible
★★★	1970 Mach 1
★★★★	1970 Boss 302
★★★★★	1970 Boss 429
Add ★	With 428CJ

Impressive as the Mustang line-up was in 1969, sales lagged behind those in 1968, and 1968 had been considerably less successful than 1967 model-year sales. Obviously, added competition in and the stabilization (and beginning decline) of the pony car market hurt Mustang sales. Still, the Mustang outsold all other pony cars. You may

The 1970 Mach 1 still looked great. The Mach 1 came with this type of grille simulating foglamps. The side scoops were deleted on all 1970 Mustang SportsRoof models.

67

Rear taillight panel and lights were changed to this configuration. Exhaust outlets were oval.

wonder, if sales were in decline, why did Ford keep bringing out more specialized Mustangs, particularly high-performance Mustangs? Besides maintaining market share, a manufacturer tries to encourage customer loyalty. A prospective buyer may be attracted by a Mach 1, but will hopefully leave the dealership a proud owner of a Ford product, even if it isn't a Mustang.

The top Mach 1 engine was the 428CJ-R with the Shaker. This one has some minor ignition improvements.

The year 1970 saw some minor juggling of the option list, plus styling revisions to differentiate the car from the 1969s. In terms of performance, there was plenty for the enthusiast to choose from.

The most obvious styling change was the front grille, which reverted to dual headlights. The lights, however, were located within the grille opening. The taillights were recessed in a flat rear taillight panel, and the simulated side scoops on the SportsRoof were deleted as on the 1969 Boss 302, resulting in a cleaner look. The simulated side vent, which had a tacky look to it, was also deleted from the hardtop and convertibles. Overall, the 1970 Mustang looked a little more sedate than did the mean 1969s.

To enhance the image of even the plainest Mustang, Sports Slats, rear wing and Shaker hood scoop were now available as separate options. Naturally the slats and wing were only available on the SportsRoof, while the Shaker could be had in any Mustang body style as long as engine size was 351 ci or larger.

The interior remained essentially the same, but the high-back bucket seats became standard equipment. Only one fancy interior option was available, the Decor Group. It included simulated wood appliques on the

Rather than having a blacked-out hood, the 1970 Mach 1s came with this stripe arrangement with the engine size on each side of the scoop, whether it was the Shaker or the simulated scoop.

Aluminum rocker panel covers replaced the side stripes of 1969.

Taillights were recessed on all 1970 Mustangs. Mach 1s also got this honeycomb treatment.

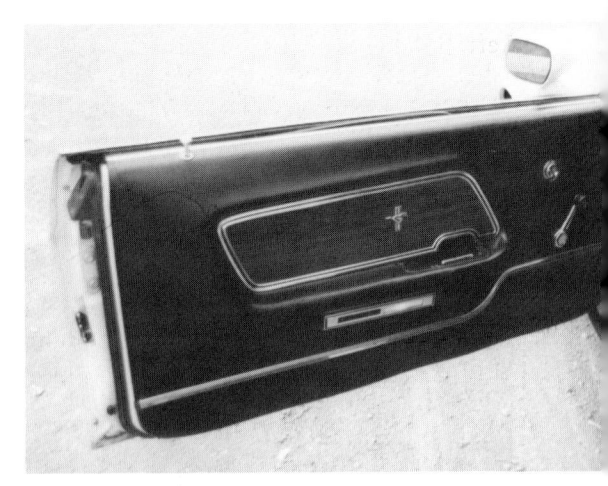

The attractive molded door panels were part of the Deluxe Interior.

dash and door panels, deluxe steering wheel, dual color-keyed racing mirrors and rocker panel, and wheel opening moldings. A noticeable change was the relocation of the ignition switch to the steering column. This was an industry-wide move designed to deter

The Deluxe Interior was still standard on the 1970 Mach 1 and Grande. The redesigned steering wheel was the most noticeable change.

theft. It didn't do much deterring, however. Other interior alterations involved detail changes to accommodate such things as different seatbelts.

Ford made some important mechanical changes. Mustangs equipped with dual exhausts got a more conventional system with two mufflers rather than the single transverse muffler used in years before. A rear stabilizer bar was added to the Competition Suspension package to improve handling. This was a bar measuring ½ inch on the 351 Mustangs, while the 428s got a ⅝ inch rear bar. The front bar on the Mach 1s measured $^{15}/_{16}$ inch. Another minor change that benefited handling was the switch to seven-inch-wide rims on the Mach 1s.

Engine line-up was identical to that of the 1969s, with the exception of two changes. The old 390 was finally retired, but more significantly, a new 351 joined the option list. This was the 351 Cleveland (351C), which shared the same bore and stroke as the 351W. In reality, it was a completely different engine. The design of the cylinder head made the engine what it was, and the 351C had the best-designed heads of any Ford factory V-8, short of a Hemi. It is true that Chevrolet pioneered the canted-valve head design, but Ford further refined it.

Unlike the 351W and other small-blocks, the 351C was designed with two separate cylinder heads, known as the two-barrel and four-barrel heads. The more common 2V head had smaller ports and valves (2.04 intake, 1.65 exhaust) and nonadjustable rocker arms. All 2V heads had an open combustion chamber design for low compression and emission. The 4V heads had much larger ports and valves (2.19 intake, 1.71 exhaust) and the 1970–71 versions have closed or quench-type combustion chambers. In fact, the 4V heads were very similar to the Boss 302 heads. Besides the larger ports and valves, the 4V heads also came

Grande interiors could be identified by this special hound's-tooth pattern upholstery.

Grande Mustangs were basically spruced up hardtops. On the exterior, they could be identified by this lettering on the C pillars.

Base wheel covers were standard equipment on the Grande.

The Grabber SportsRoof was basically a specially striped SportsRoof. This one has a side stripe similar to the one on the 1969 Boss 302.

with cylinder blocks that had four-bolt mains.

Even the 2V heads outflowed the 351W by a wide margin. The 2V version, with its 9:1 compression ratio and 350 cfm two-barrel carburetor, was rated at 250 hp at 4600 rpm. The 4V engine, with a 470 cfm carburetor and 11:1 compression, was rated by Ford at 300 hp at 5400 rpm.

The 428s remained unchanged; however, you could now order the Drag Pack option

The 351W was still available on 1970 Mustangs, but only in two-barrel form.

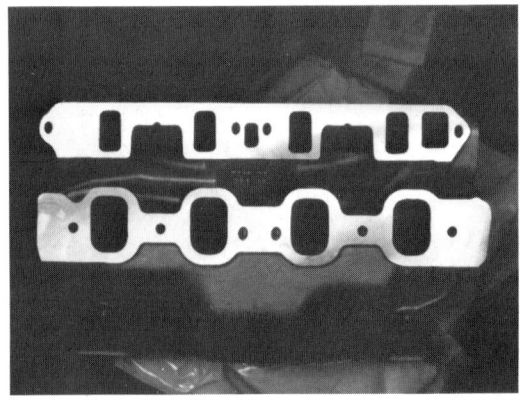

A comparison of intake ports on the 351W(top) and 351C-4V(bottom) shows the difference in power potential between the two engines.

The 1970 Boss 302 was relatively unchanged. Chrome Magnum 500 wheels were now optional. This example has all the desirable Boss 302 options, rear deck spoiler, slats and shaker hood scoop.

Shaker Scoop was optional on all 1970 Boss 302s.

1970 Boss 302 from the rear.

The trim rings and hubcaps on 15×7 steel wheels were standard equipment on the Boss 302. Chrome Magnum 500s were optional.

group with the 428CJ-R engine, which effectively transformed the engine to a 428SCJ. As in 1969, it came with a 3.91:1 or 4.30:1 axle ratio, engine oil cooler and stronger connecting rods.

Transmission choices remained the same in 1970, although all four-speeds now came with a Hurst shifter and T-handle.

Specials

The only change in model line-up was the deletion of the GT Equipment Group—no more Mustang GTs (until 1982, that is). The Grande got some changes: the interior got a hound's tooth pattern on the seats and a half-vinyl roof. A full vinyl roof was optional. Also new was the addition of a plastic rear taillight panel.

The appearance of the Mach 1 changed. The rocker panels were covered with a full-length aluminum cover and had large Mach 1 lettering on the front. The blacked-out hood disappeared; a hood with black or white stripes with engine size numbers around the hood scoop took its place. The simulated hood scoop, painted black, was standard equipment on all Mach 1s, but the Shaker, as mentioned earlier, was optional with the 351 engines. The NASCAR-type hood-pins were replaced by twist-type click units. The Mach 1 grille received two Sportlamps which enhanced the appearance of the Mach 1 more than anything else. The Sportlamps made the 1970 Mach 1 resemble the more aggressive look of the 1969 model. The rear taillight area got a honeycomb-design panel, and the tail stripe was enlarged and had much larger Mach 1 lettering.

Other visual changes were the mag-style hubcaps mounted on 14×7 inch steel wheels and chrome oval exhaust tips for the four-barrel engines. Black-painted styled steel wheels were a no-cost option.

The interior of the Mach 1 still had woodgrain appliques on the doors, dash, console and steering wheel.

The 428CJ Mach 1s were still probably as fast as you could go in the quarter-mile in a street car. Competition, however, was getting stronger. Pontiac came out with a 455 ci Trans Am model. And of course, Chrysler, almost six years after the Mustang was introduced, finally fielded its own true pony cars; the Barracuda and the Challenger with the 440 six Pack or the 426 Chrysler Hemi

Most Boss 302s came with the standard interior.

Standard Boss 302 engine now came with aluminum valve covers.

75

> **1970 Mach 1 Mustang**
> SportsRoof body
> 250 hp 351W or 351C V-8; optional engines: 300 hp 351C, 335 hp 428CJ
> 3-speed manual transmission
> Competition Suspension (heavier springs, shocks, front and rear sway bars)
> Deluxe interior with center console, Rim-Blow Deluxe steering wheel, electric clock, high-back bucket seats
> Color-keyed dual racing mirrors
> Twist-type hood latches
> Nonfunctional hood scoop
> Center of hood painted either black or white, with tape stripe border and engine size numerals
> Grille-mounted Sportlamps
> Honeycomb rear panel with Mach 1 tape stripe on rear deck lid
> Dual exhaust system with chrome oval extensions (optional engines only)
> Pop-open gas cap
> Aluminum Mach 1 rocker panel molding
> Sports wheel covers or Argent styled steel wheels
> E70×14 WSW tires (F70×14 RWL on 428CJ)
> **Desirable options**
> 4-speed manual or 3-speed automatic transmission
> 428CJ Ram Air engine with Shaker scoop
> Traction Lok differential
> Drag Pack (includes 428SCJ Ram Air engine, Shaker scoop, 3.91:1 or 4.30:1 axle ratio, engine oil cooler)
> Sports Slats
> Rear deck spoiler
> Shaker hood scoop with 351 engines
> Power disc brakes
> Power steering
> Air conditioning
> Fold-down rear seat

were real brutes, but they were a lot heavier than the Mustang. All pony cars were limited by tire technology.

Boss 302

Production of the Boss 302 continued in 1970 with some slight changes that made it a

You'll need sunglasses to look at Alec Garden's Weber carbureted Boss 302!

This is what a Shaker-equipped 1970 Boss 302 engine compartment looks like, although many components have been chromed by its owner.

better car. Ford chose to put more effort behind its promotional campaign, and sales hit a high of 7,013 units.

The 1970 Boss 302 used the SportsRoof body with the color-keyed mirrors and front spoiler. Occasionally, you may see a Boss 302 without the front spoiler, and this is because it was never installed. These cars were shipped to the dealers without the spoiler installed. It was up to the dealers to install it, and apparently, dealers didn't always do so.

Exterior color selection expanded with the addition of the bright Grabber color series. The rear deck and taillight area remained blacked-out, but the side C-stripes were eliminated. They were replaced by a hood stripe flanked with two smaller stripes that turned at the fender and went along the sides of the car, incorporating the Boss 302 lettering.

Other visual changes included the 15×7 inch wheels that used an aluminum hubcap and trim ring combination, although the handsome chrome Magnum 500 wheels were optional. Tire size was still F60×15. In

Another mouth-watering sight was this owner-installed Weber-equipped 351 Cleveland.

77

The ultimate Boss 302s were the ones that were actually raced in the Trans Am Series. Compared to today's race cars, the Boss 302 looks almost stock. Dale Sale

addition, the rear wing and Sports Slats and the Shaker hood scoop became an option on the Boss 302, and some 302s even had a hood-mounted tachometer. As with other Mustangs, the Boss 302 got the high-back bucket seats as standard equipment, and while most still got the standard interior, the Decor Group was optional.

The engine received some minor modifications that tended to improve performance. Intake valve size was reduced to 2.19 inches from 2.23 inches. Even the 2.19 inch valves were too large for a street engine measuring 302 ci—for example, the Chevrolet 454 ci big-block used a 2.19 inch intake valve, and the 302 ci Z-28 motor got along with just 2.02 inches. The large valves helped engine breathing over 6500 rpm. Other changes included the substitution of the cross-drilled crankshaft for a unit that was not cross-drilled. Apparently, it made no difference in a street engine and enabled Ford to save a few dollars. The chrome valve covers were replaced by finned aluminum versions, although some early 1970 Boss 302s had chrome covers.

The Boss 302 also got the dual-muffler exhaust system, a ½ inch rear sway bar, a front bar of $15/16$ inch and the Hurst shifter for crisper shifts.

The year 1970 marked the end of Boss 302 production. The SCCA changed the rules for the 1971 Trans-Am season, allowing engines with a maximum displacement of 350 ci. This prompted Ford to drop the expensive Boss 302 and to replace it with the Boss 351. Ford of Canada did build a few 1971 Boss 302s, although no exact figures are available.

A 1970 Boss 429, with its simple, understated look. Dane Miller

---

1970 Boss 302 Mustang
SportsRoof body
Color-keyed dual racing mirrors
Front spoiler
Boss 302 hood to side stripes
Low-gloss black paint on rear deck lid and taillight panel
Brushed aluminum hubcaps and trim rings on 15X7-inch steel wheels with F60X15 RWL Goodyear Polyglas GT tires
290 hp Boss 302 engine with finned aluminum valve covers, aluminum intake manifold, Holley 780 cfm carburetor, electronic rev-limiter, dual exhaust system
4-speed manual transmission with Hurst shifter
Quick-ratio steering
Power front disc brakes
3.50:1 rear axle ratio
Staggered rear shock absorbers and rear sway bar
High-back bucket seats
Desirable options
Deluxe interior with console
Fold-down rear seat
Rear deck spoiler
Rear window slats
Shaker hood scoop
Chrome Magnum 500 15X7 inch wheels
8000 rpm tachometer
Power steering
Traction Lok differential

All 1970 Boss 429s came with black-painted hood scoops. *Steve Dowdall*

The 1970 Boss 429 engine benefited from a better camshaft and exhaust system. This is another modified engine.

In spite of the fact that significantly more 1970 Boss 302s were built, there doesn't seem to be much of a dollar difference between the two years in terms of collector prices. If you are interested in one, I would suggest you get one that has a rebuilt engine because of the piston problem.

The Boss 302 represents a high point for the first-generation Mustangs. It combined handling, braking and acceleration in a visually exciting package.

Boss 429

The 1970 Boss 429 remained essentially the same, receiving only minor body and mechanical changes. Unlike the Boss 302, production of the Boss 429 declined to 499 units. It should also be noted that all Boss 429 Mustangs were built from January to December 1969, with a short break in the

The 1970 Boss 429s came with either the standard interior or the optional deluxe interior. The Hurst shifter was standard equipment. *Steve Dowdall*

The composite Quarter Horse was a prototype that combined features of the Boss 429 (engine and chassis) with a Shelby nose and an interior that had a Cougar dash. Although Ford designed this other pony as a possible mid-year replacement for the Boss 429 and Shelby Mustangs, plans were shelved as interest in performance cars waned. *Ford Motor Company*

summer to accommodate the model changeover.

Besides the 1970 Mustang body changes, the 1970 Boss 429 can be distinguished by its black hood scoop, regardless of body color. Exterior color choice expanded and included the Grabber colors. The Boss 429 continued to use the chrome Magnum 500 wheels, although these now had a small center hubcap like the Boss 302.

Only one Boss 429 engine was available, the T series. Some of these were tagged A as they had minor modifications to the emission system. The major change was the use of a mechanical lifter camshaft, the same unit found on the 429SCJ wedge engine, which was supposed to increase horsepower by thirty at 6000 rpm. The engine, however, was still rated at 375 hp.

The only suspension change was the use of a Boss 302 type rear sway bar measuring ⅝ inch, mounted over the rear axle.

1970 Boss 429 Mustang
SportsRoof body
Color-keyed dual racing mirrors
Front spoiler
Boss 429 fender decals
Gloss-black hood scoop
Boss 429 375 hp V-8 engine with aluminum cylinder heads, intake manifold and valve covers
Engine oil cooler
Power steering
4-speed close-ratio manual transmission with Hurst shifter
Power disc brakes
Trunk-mounted battery
Special High Performance suspension with front and rear sway bars, staggered rear shock absorbers
Chrome 15×7-inch Magnum 500 wheels with F60×15 Goodyear Polyglas GT RWL tires, Boss 302 style hubcap
3.91:1 Traction Lok differential
8000 rpm tachometer
AM radio
Desirable options
Deluxe interior with console

Inside, the base Mustang interior was standard equipment, while the Decor Group was optional.

The limited edition Twister Special sported distinctive stripes and Twister decals. *Terry Fritts*

81

According to the Boss 429 Registry, 451 1969 Boss 429s and 253 1970 models have been located after some ten years of searching. I am sure that there are a few units out there unaccounted for, but it seems that the bulk of these rare cars have been found.

Incidentally, Ford built two Boss 429 Cougars. There were also two Quarter Horse prototypes, which have been located. The Quarter Horse was a 1970 Mustang that used a Shelby nose with the Boss 429 engine, but it never reached production.

Another Boss 429 variant was a unique mid-engined 1970 Mustang, with the engine mounted behind the rear seat. There is reason to believe that this car exists because it was not sent to the crusher, as was the normal procedure for prototype cars at Ford engineering.

Prospects

The Boss 429s are Mustangs without equal, simply for their extremely large and complex engines. They are probably the most valuable production Mustang as they satisfy all the prerequisites for collectorship: low production, historical significance and uniqueness.

From an investment angle, all Boss 429s will continue to appreciate at a much faster rate than will other Mustangs. Originality is much more important here, since any missing special Boss 429 parts (and there are a lot of special parts) are extremely difficult to replace. And due to their low production, to reproduce them is uneconomical for anyone.

Even though originality is important, you'll find many modified Boss 429 Mustangs. Usually these will have even rarer race or prototype parts such as exotic induction systems made in small quantities. These cars live up to the potential of the Boss 429 engine.

You'll also find many of these cars have the rear wing and Sports Slats although they weren't available at the time as an option from Ford. Not original in the strictest sense, these items really enhance the car's image.

Offering tremendous acceleration and handling to match, the Boss 429 represented the high point in big-block Mustangs and exemplified the extreme to which manufacturers went in their quest for supremacy on the track.

Worth mentioning, too, are the Grabber SportsRoof Mustangs that were available in 1970. If you wanted to enhance the appearance of a base SportsRoof, you could order your Mustang with the Grabber side stripes. There were two versions: one looked exactly like the 1969 Boss 302 side stripes but without the 302 lettering, and the other looked like a hockey stick. These incorporated either 302 or 351 numerals for engine size. Most of these Mustangs came with the hub cap and trim ring combination.

In 1970 Ford still produced special Mustangs for specific areas of the country. One of the more interesting was the Twister Special made for the Kansas City District. The Twister Special consisted of a group of ninety-six consecutively produced and numbered Mach 1s, all painted Grabber Orange. The sides of the car got a unique side stripe, while the rear fenders got the Twister decal. Forty-eight of these were equipped with the 428SCJ engine, while the other forty-eight came with the 351C four-barrel engine.

The 1970 Mustangs, along with the 1969 models, are gaining in popularity. There is quite a lot to choose from if you are looking for a performance Mustang, and with the exception of the rarer Boss 429s and 302s, there are quite a few cars still out there. The 428 Mustangs are starting to inch up. You'll note that only 2,671 Mustangs came with this monster engine in 1970. Both 1969 and 1970 models are better driving cars than are their predecessors, and they still look a lot like the early Mustangs, which is important to many people. Because of such characteristics, these Mustangs will, I think, generate considerable activity among collectors.

Chapter 7

1971-72 Mustangs

★✓	1971-72 Hardtop
★★	1971-72 Fastback
★★★	1971-72 Convertible
★★★✓	1971-72 Mach 1
★★★★	1971 Boss 351
Add ★	With 429CJ/ SCJ

1971
The year 1971 saw the last major restyle of the first-generation Mustang. While maintaining the original's proportions, the Mustang grew in every dimension except height. Wheelbase increased to 109 inches; track grew by 3 inches, length by 2.1 inches and weight by about 200 pounds. When compared to a 1965 Mustang, the changes were far more obvious. The 1971 was longer,

This 1971 convertible has the standard grille. Big car look is accentuated by the Mustang's large hood. *Ford Motor Company*

A typical fully optioned 1971 Mach 1 had front and rear spoilers, Magnum 500 wheels and one of the larger V-8s.

NASA ducts on the hood replaced the previous hood scoops. Foglamps are owner installed.

This 1972 SportsRoof, with aftermarket wheels, shows the almost flat rear window. *Paul McLaughlin*

wider and heavier, by about 800 pounds. It was even styled to create the illusion that it was larger. From the interior, the hood looked absolutely massive, yet the car was only 0.5 inch longer and slightly narrower than the redesigned 1970 Camaro. In part,

The smallest V-8 available during 1971-73 was a 302 two-barrel. The small radiator in front of the valve cover was for the power steering.

the Mustang's size increased to accommodate the large 429 engines. But I also feel that the concept that bigger is better, which was the American auto industry's prevailing theme until the early eighties, was responsible as well.

On the other hand, the new Mustangs were much smoother, more sophisticated and mechanically up-to-date than previous Mustangs. Mustangs had never been more luxurious either.

Ford still built the Mustang in three configurations: hardtop, convertible and SportsRoof. The most noticeable change was the flat front grille, which retained the dual headlights. The wipers were hidden, and the windshield was tilted back even more than before. On the SportsRoof, the rear window angle was only fourteen degrees from horizontal, which resulted in a cleaner aerodynamic look; it was also a lot harder to see out.

For the first time, a vinyl roof option was available on the SportsRoof.

The interior was redesigned as well. The dash now used a three-pod arrangement, which consisted of a fuel gauge in the center pod and a speedometer in the right-hand pod. All other functions were relegated to the left pod, which consisted of warning lights.

More interesting was the optional instrumentation. The warning lights on the left pod were replaced by an 8000 rpm tachometer, and a panel with three gauges (oil pressure, amps and temperature) was placed just above the radio.

The bucket seats, which look similar to the 1970's were also redesigned. Important interior options included: full-length console, electric rear window defroster (except on convertibles) tilt steering wheel, three-spoke Rim-Blow steering wheel, fold-down

For more reasonable street performance, one of the many 351Cs was desirable. This one has Ram Air.

rear seat, air conditioning and, for the first time, power windows.

Buyers chose from two interior option groups. The Decor Group came with knitted vinyl or cloth seats, door panels with wood appliques, deluxe two-spoke steering wheel, dual color-keyed mirrors, and chrome rocker panels and wheelwell moldings. The Mach 1 Sports Interior, which came with the Mach 1, was optional on any SportsRoof Mustang. It included a different upholstery on the seats, the deluxe steering wheel and door panels, the instrument group, an electric clock and a special carpet with integral rubber floor mats.

The base engine was the 250 ci six-cylinder rated at 145 hp. Two transmissions were available, either a three-speed manual or a three-speed automatic. This was followed by 210 hp 302 two-barrel, 240 hp 351C two-barrel, 285 hp 351C four-barrel and two 429s rated at 370 hp and 375 hp respectively. Only the four-barrel 351C and 429s came with the four-speed manual as standard; the automatic was optional.

Late in the model year, another 351C engine was released. This was the 351CJ rated at 280 hp, and with a lower compression ratio of 8.6:1.

The most interesting engine in 1971 was the 429. The 429, a destroked version of the 460 that powered Lincolns, made its first appearance in a 1968 Thunderbird. This was Ford's answer to the big-block Chevrolet engine, and it was similar in design, but compared to the Chevy, featured refined cylinder head port configuration. The 429 was also designed to be a cleaner engine, producing fewer emissions than the FE series engines it replaced. When the 429/460 was designed, Ford was also looking to a future that never materialized. For example, there were plans for a 501 ci version, initially for use in the big luxury cars.

Mustangs could be had with three versions of the 429. The 429CJ, the 429CJ-R (Ram Air) and the 429SCJ-R. All these used large intake and exhaust valves (2.25 and 1.72 inches respectively) and had an 11.3:1 compression ratio and the large-port cylinder heads. Like the 351C, the 429 was available with two sets of heads. The small-port, small-valved heads were used in non-performance applications and none of these were ever installed in a Mustang. The 429CJ and 429CJ-R were rated at 370 hp at 5400 rpm. They used a hydraulic cam, and some early versions had adjustable rocker arms. More importantly, the CJ came with four-bolt main caps for increased durability. In an unusual move, both the 429CJ and 429CJ-R came with a Rochester Quadrajet carburetor, flowing 700 cfm.

All functional Ram Air hoods came with appropriate decals.

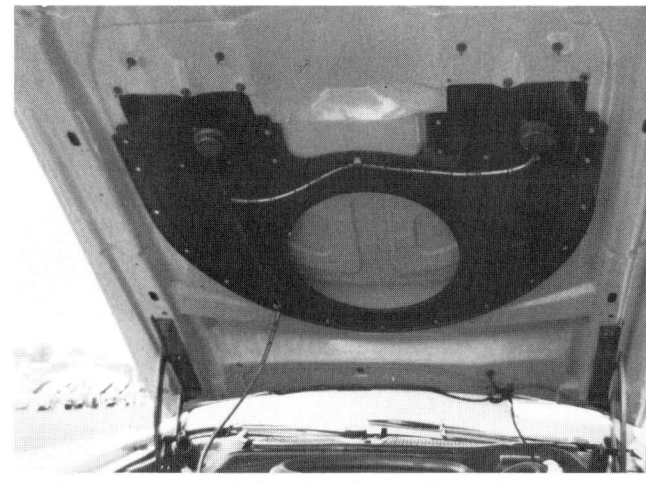

Underhood look of the functional Ram Air setup.

The fold-down rear seat was still available on the restyled 1971-73 Mustangs.

The most powerful engine available was the 429SCJ-R. Available only with the Drag Pack option, which meant either a 3.91:1 Traction Lok or 4.11:1 Detroit Locker rear, it was rated at only five horsepower more than the 429CJ. Internally, the 429SCJ-R was modified and strengthened to cope with the extra power it produced. A higher performance mechanical camshaft with adjustable rocker arms and a Holley 780 cfm carburetor replaced the Quadrajet. The 429SCJ-R also used stronger forged pistons. The oil cooler was not part of the Drag Pack option, although you'll run into some cars that have it.

The 429s were available with a close-ratio four-speed or the C-6 automatic. Power steering and power brakes were mandatory with these heavyweights. Speaking of power steering, Mustangs with the optional Competition Suspension used a variable-ratio steering box made by GM.

Only 1,255 Mustangs were built with the 429CJ and 429CJ-R engines, and even fewer with the 429SCJ-R: 610 units.

Specials

The Grande was again available in 1971, catering to those interested in a luxury hardtop. The Grande came with a standard vinyl roof, a gussied-up interior that included the deluxe two-spoke steering wheel and instrument panel appliques, rocker panel and wheelwell opening moldings, color-keyed mirrors and appropriate Grande identification.

Mach 1

The performance Mustang was the Mach 1. The package included color-keyed rearview mirrors, unique honeycomb front grille with integral Sportlamps, color-keyed bumper unique to the Mach 1, redesigned gas cap, Mach 1 fender decals, Mach 1 rear deck lid stripe, honeycomb taillight panel, and black- or Argent-painted lower body areas depending on the exterior color. The front and rear valence panels were similarly painted. The four-barrel 351s and all 429s

Trunk on the fastback was ridiculously small, considering the size and weight of the Mustang.

These are the upgraded door panels.

88

This 1971 Mach 1 interior has the optional instrument cluster and console.

came with dual exhaust extensions. The NASA hood was a no-cost option on the Mach 1 with the base engine and standard equipment on all other engines. Having the NASA hood did not mean that the Mustang was equipped with Ram Air. Hoods with functional Ram Air came with Ram Air

Standard Mach 1 wheels during 1971-73 were 14×6 inch steel wheels with trim rings and hubcaps.

Optional during 1971-72 were the 15×7 chrome Magnum 500 wheels.

The 429CJ powered Mustangs were the last big-block Mustangs. *Marvin Scothorn*

Although the big 429CJ engine was available on all Mustang body styles, the majority of these were found on the Mach 1. *Bobby Spedale*

decals on either side of the scoops. Unlike in previous Mach 1s, the standard interior was the base Mustang interior. The fancier Mach 1 Sports Interior was optional.

Standard Mach 1 wheels were the brushed aluminum trim rings and hubcaps sporting whitewall E70×14 tires with the 302 and 351 cars, while the 429s came with RWL F70×14 tires. Optional and more desirable were the 15×7 Chrome Magnum 500 wheels with Goodyear F60×15 RWL tires. All Mach 1s came with the Competition Suspension, which had the usual heavier-duty springs and shocks and 7/8 inch front and 1/2 inch rear sway bars. The 429 Mach 1s (and other Mustangs powered by this engine) came with a larger 5/8 inch rear bar.

The base engine on the Mach 1 was the 302, which really wasn't enough engine for a Mustang evoking such a racer image. The two-barrel 351 was next on the option list, but for passable street performance, the 285 hp four-barrel 351 was necessary.

The only way you could identify 429-powered Mach 1s was from the hood decals.

With the 429CJ, straightline performance was more than acceptable, mid- to high-thirteen seconds in the quarter-mile. Like

The 429CJ-R used a Rochester Quadrajet carburetor.

The 429SCJ-R used a 780 Holley four-barrel carburetor. All 429s came with finned aluminum valve covers. *Craig Comjean*

1971 Mustang Mach 1
SportsRoof body
210 hp V-8; optional engines: 240 hp 351C, 385 hp 351C, 370 hp 429CJ-R, 375 hp 429SCJ-R
3-speed manual transmission
Power variable-ratio steering
Competition Suspension (includes front and rear sway bars)
Nonfunctional NASA hood with twist-type lock pins
Honeycomb front grille and color-keyed bumper
Honeycomb rear panel with pop-open gas cap
Black or Argent lower body panels
Black or Argent hood
Color-keyed dual racing mirrors
Mach 1 fender decals
Mach 1 lettering on rear deck lid
Brushed aluminum wheel covers and trim rings
Dual exhaust system with round chrome outlets (with 4V-equipped engines)
Desirable options
4-speed manual or 3-speed automatic transmission
Power disc brakes
429CJ-R or 429SCJ-R engines
Traction Lok differential
Mach 1 Sports Interior (includes console, clock, triple instrument pod, high-back bucket seats)
Deluxe three-spoke Rim-Blow steering wheel
Rear deck spoiler
Power side windows
Fold-down rear seat
15×7 inch chrome Magnum 500 wheels with F60×15 RWL tires
Air conditioning
Side and rear deck stripes
Front spoiler

most big-block Mustangs, handling, when pushed hard, was not good. A nice set of modern radial tires will make a tremendous difference—provided you aren't into strict originality—as will some minor suspension tuning.

The last of the Boss series Mustangs, the Boss 351. *Randy Ream*

Looking similar to the Mach 1, the Boss 351 combined good handling with excellent acceleration. *Brent Galloway*

Boss 351

The last Boss Mustang built was the Boss 351, and it too, lived up to the Boss concept of a car that would accelerate, brake and handle with the best that Detroit could offer. In stock form, the Boss 351 equaled or surpassed the acceleration of other big-block Mustangs (and other pony cars), and its weight distribution provided better handling and braking. Like its predecessors, the Boss 351 was a complete package, with few options.

Fender and rear deck decals were all that identified the Boss 351.

A few Boss 351s came with a hood paint scheme like the Mach 1's. All Boss 351s came with chrome front bumpers.

The Boss 351 used the Mach 1 Sports-Roof, with some differences. The functional NASA hood was standard equipment, but the Boss 351 used a chrome front bumper rather than the color-keyed bumper of the Mach 1. The hood, rocker panels, and front and rear valence panels were black or Argent to contrast with the exterior paint color, and all Boss 351s used a front spoiler.

The Boss 351 used the standard Mustang interior, but the three-pod instrument package was standard equipment. Other interiors were optional.

The Boss 351 had a unique side stripe and small Boss 351 decals on the fenders and rear deck lid. Later in the model year, however, the Mach 1 could be optioned with these stripes as well, diluting the impact of the Boss 351.

Other standard items were the 15×7 brushed aluminum wheels with the Goodyear F60×15 tires, but the 15×7 Chrome Magnum 500 wheels were optional. The rear wing was optional, but no rear window slats were available from Ford, probably due to the almost flat angle of the rear window.

All Boss 351s came with a wide-ratio-four-speed manual that used a Hurst Shifter, a 3.91:1 rear axle ratio and the Competition Suspension with the larger 5/8 inch rear sway bar.

As with other Boss Mustangs, the heart of the Boss package was the engine. The Boss 351 was Ford's most advanced medium-block engine. Like the four-barrel 351C in the 1970 Mach 1, the Boss 351 used a four-bolt main block and the large-port, big-valve cylinder heads. Because of the mechanical lifter camshaft, however, the Boss 351 used adjustable rocker arms. The engine was also equipped with specially treated forged steel rods, and the crankshaft was specially chosen for high nodularity. The Boss 351 came with an aluminum intake manifold, but unlike previous Boss engines, it used a 750 cfm Motorcraft carburetor. Compression ratio was a high 11:1. Like the Boss 302, the

This Boss 351 got the standard interior with the optional console. The Hurst shifter was standard as well. *Randy Ream*

On the Boss 351 engine, finned valve covers distinguished it from other 351s.

The year 1972 brought us the Mustang Sprint, including this rare convertible. *Jerome Holiber*

Most Mustang Sprints were either hardtops or SportsRoofs. This convertible is one of 50 specially made. *Jerome Holiber*

Rarest of the 1972 Mustangs were those powered by the 351 HO engine, which was a slightly detuned Boss 351. All 351 HOs came with a fresh air intake system rather than Ram Air.

Boss 351 used a rev-limiter, limiting rpm to 6150.

1971 Boss 351 Mustang
SportsRoof body
Chrome front bumper
Boss 351 decals on fenders and rear deck lid
Argent or black side stripes
Argent or black lower body areas and hood
Ram Air hood decals
Functional NASA hood with twist-type lock pins
Color-keyed dual racing mirrors
Front spoiler
Brushed aluminum wheel covers and trim rings on 15X7 inch steel wheels with F60X15 tires
Dual exhaust system with chrome outlets
Boss 351 engine, 330 hp with finned aluminum valve covers, aluminum intake manifold, mechanical camshaft, electronic rev-limiter
Power front disc brakes
3.91:1 axle ratio
Traction Lok differential
Competition Suspension with staggered rear shocks, ⅝ inch rear sway bar
4-speed manual transmission with Hurst shifter
Standard Mustang interior with 3-pod instrumentation group (oil, temperature and ampere gauges)
High-back bucket seats
Desirable options
15X7 chrome Magnum 500 wheels
Rear deck spoiler
Mach 1 Sports Interior
Power steering
Fold-down rear seat

Ford rated this 351 at 330 hp at 5400 rpm. Considering the high-thirteen- to low-fourteen-second quarter-mile times and the weight of the car (3,750 pounds), Ford was obviously underrating the output of this engine.

Overall, the Boss 351 handled better than the Mach 1s because it had large tires and slightly bigger rear sway bar. It could out-accelerate other cars with much bigger engines and had much better low-end response than did previous Boss Mustangs.

Only 1,806 Boss 351 Mustangs were built. These trail other Bosses in value because of the larger 1971 body style, but they still are a worthwhile investment.

Later in the model year, Ford further diluted the performance image of the Mach 1 and Boss 351 by offering features from both cars on the hardtop. This was the Sports Hardtop that used the Mach 1 grille, NASA hood, color-keyed front bumper, Boss 351 side stripes, lower body paint, and color-keyed mirrors. It may have helped hardtop sales, but it clearly showed that Ford was using any means possible, even at the expense of performance, to promote sales.

1972

The 1972 Mustangs stand out simply because they don't stand out. Besides minor changes, it is difficult to spot the differences between a 1971 and a 1972. For the first time, the Mustang's basic styling went unchanged as Ford concentrated more on meeting emission and safety regulations. Also, development of the Mustang II was well along the way.

Although the Mustang looked the same, some changes were made, particularly under the hood. The Boss 351 model was dropped, as were the big-block 429s. The top engine was the 351CJ, which was introduced in late 1971. Rated at 266 hp, using the SAE net rating, it was still a respectable engine, even though the compression ratio was dropped

The Grande hardtop continued to be promoted as the luxury Mustang. *Ford Motor Company*

The 1972 Mustang Sprints in either hardtop or SportsRoof form definitely stood out. *Ford Motor Company*

The Sprint package consisted of unique interior trim and exterior graphics. *Ford Motor Company*

to 8.8:1. It still came equipped with the better 351 4V heads.

Next in line, was the two-barrel 351C rated at 177 hp, while the two-barrel 302 managed to pump out 140 hp. The standard engine, the 250 ci six, put out 98 hp.

Briefly during the beginning of the model year, however, Ford made one last gasp at performance. This was the limited 351 HO (for High Output), which was available with any Mustang body. Basically, the 351 HO was a detuned version of the 1971 Boss 351 engine. It was rated at 275 hp at 6000 rpm. All the good pieces of the Boss 351 were included, but the compression ratio was reduced to 8.8:1 so that the engine could run on regular gas.

Mandatory options with the 351 HO were power front disc brakes, Competition Suspension, wide-ratio four-speed manual transmission, 3.91:1 Traction Lok rear axle and F60×15 RWL Goodyears on 15×7 wheels. Quarter-mile times were recorded at 15.1 seconds at 95.6 mph and 0–60 mph at 6.6 seconds, by *Car and Driver* magazine. About 1,000 Mustangs were so equipped, making them the last true performance Mustangs of the first generation.

Noteworthy changes on the 1972 are as follows. The Exterior Decor Group, available on hardtops and convertibles, consisted of the Mach 1 grille and Sportslamps, color-keyed front bumper, lower body paint treatment, special moldings, and brushed aluminum trim rings and hubcaps. You could also get the Mach 1 tape stripes on convertibles. The NASA hood was still available, but the Ram Air option was limited to the 351 two-barrel engine during the second half of the model year.

The Mach 1 was unchanged from 1971, although the rear pop-open gas cap was replaced by the regular production cap. The Grande, too, was unchanged, with the exception of different side stripes.

Only one new model was introduced in 1972, the Sprint. The Sprint featured a special exterior paint treatment to coordinate with a unique interior. It was not a performance package by any means and was available on hardtops and fastbacks. All Sprints

---

1972 Mach 1 Mustang
Identical to 1971 Mach 1 except:
Pop-open gas cap deleted
429CJ-R, 429SCJ-R engines deleted
1972 engines
140 hp 302 ci V-8; optional engines: 177 hp 351C, 266 hp 351CJ, 275 hp 351 HO
Dual exhaust system with round chrome outlets on 351CJ and 351 HO engines
Desirable options
351 HO engine, includes following mandatory options: 4-speed manual transmission, power steering, 15×7 inch Magnum 500 wheels with F60×15 tires

---

were painted white with red and blue stripes on the hood, rear panel and lower body area. A USA shield decal was placed on the rear quarter panel—patriotic indeed. All Sprints came with the Exterior Decor Group, dual color-keyed mirrors and E70×14 whitewall tires on wheels with brushed aluminum trim rings and hubcaps. This Sprint combination was known as Sprint Package A. Package B replaced the fourteen-inch wheels with the 15×7 Chrome Magnum 500s, using the F60×15 RWL Goodyear tires.

There was, however, a special run of fifty Sprint convertibles made for Washington, D. C. These were used in the Cherry Day Parade, and each car represented one state.

Incidentally, any 1972 Mustang that came with the Magnum 500 wheels also had to have the Competition Suspension as it was a mandatory option.

Prospects

Obviously, the most collectible 1971s were the Boss 351s and the 429-powered Mach 1s. However, convertibles as in previous model years, are also highly collectible; the more options, the better. As in earlier Mustangs, rust is just as much of a problem, but the availability of reproduction body panels is limited. The same applies for most of the interior trim and upholstery. It is much more of a challenge to restore a 1971–73 Mustang.

It is true that the 1971–73 Mustangs may be the least popular of the first-generation Mustangs, but they do have a solid core of support. They can also be a good alternative to some of the pricier early Mustangs.

Of all the 1972 Mustangs, the 351 HO Mustangs hold some special significance because they are the last true high-performance Mustangs of the first generation. However, they are quite rare.

In 1972, sales for the Mustang continued to slide, reflecting the downward trend in the pony car market. Still, the Mustang ran number one, ahead of all other pony cars.

Chapter 8

★★	1973 Hardtop
★★	1973 Fastback
★★★	1973 Convertible
★★★	1973 Mach 1

1973 Mustangs

The last year for the big-bodied Mustang was 1973. Although restyled slightly, it was not very different from the 1972. The Mustang had grown too big and thus alienated much of its customer base. Cars like the Maverick, Chevy Nova and Plymouth Duster were selling well, and in many ways they were closer to the original Mustang, at least in terms of size. Part of the original's allure was its right size: it was trim and compact, while the later Mustangs were on their way to becoming an intermediate. The Cougar, by 1973, had already graduated to intermediate size, giving up all pretense of being a pony car.

In fact, Ford's German-built Capri was enjoying modest success, while the car that captured the hearts of many enthusiasts was the Datsun 240Z. Ford would try to bring back those who left with the advent of the 1974 Mustang II, but in the meantime there was still the 1973 Mustang.

Mustang evolution is obvious from this comparison of a 1965 Shelby and a 1973 Mach 1. *Brent Galloway*

The 1973 Mach 1 came with different side stripes and a different grille. *Brent Galloway*

Fourteen inch forged aluminum wheels took the place of the Magnum 500s as the top wheel option. *Brent Galloway*

The most noticeable exterior change was the new grille, which used vertical parking lights at each end. All 1973 Mustangs used a color-keyed front bumper designed to pass the new (for 1973) 5 mph crash test. Considering that most 1973 cars sported big battering rams for bumpers, Ford did a nice job on the Mustang. Rear bumper standards weren't quite so strict yet, but the chrome rear bumper was mounted a little bit further from the body.

The Decor Group was still available. In place of the standard egg-crate grille was a honeycomb grille with a small Mustang emblem. The headlight bezels were also blacked-out versus chrome for standard Mustangs; Ford also used this grille on the Mach 1. The lower bodyside paint treatment and the brushed aluminum trim ring and hubcap combination rounded out the package.

The side tape stripe, a Boss 351 original, was still optionally available in conjunction with the Decor Group. In this way, even the nonperformance Mustangs looked hot.

The Mach 1 Sports Interior was still available, as was the rear wing and almost all 1972 options. Noticeably absent were the 15×7 Magnum 500 wheels. Fourteen-inch forged aluminum wheels took their place on the option list.

The Mach 1 and Grande were, again, relatively unchanged. But the Mach 1 did get a new side stripe which began at the front fender and ended just before the rear wheelwell.

Engine and drivetrain combinations were unchanged. The 351CJ was the top engine option; however, it was not available with Ram Air. Only the two-barrel version of the 351 could be had with Ram Air, at extra cost of course.

Some mechanical improvements did appear in spite of 1973's being the last year for the first-generation Mustang. Suspension travel was increased by a negligible ¼

The last of the first generation convertibles was this 1973.

103

inch, and the standard drum brakes were larger, mainly due to government regulations. The convertible was now equipped with power front disc brakes as standard.

Even with the 351CJ, it was clear that performance no longer mattered. For example, a 1965 Mustang with the 271 hp 289 would out-accelerate the last big Mustang. At least these 1973 Mustangs had the potential for decent performance, if the usual hop-up techniques were employed.

Prospects

You'll find that 1973 Mustangs fetch slightly more than a comparable 1971 or 1972 (excluding the 1971 429s and Boss 351). This higher price reflects the cars' status as the last of the breed. The Mustang had strayed too far from its origins and had become just another car, losing the broad appeal it once had.

1973 Mach 1 Mustang
SportsRoof body
140 hp 302 ci V-8; optional engines: 177 hp 351C, 266 hp 351CJ
3-speed manual transmission
Power variable-ratio steering
Competition Suspension (includes front and rear sway bars)
Nonfunctional NASA hood with twist-type lock pins
Color-keyed front bumper
Color-keyed dual racing mirrors
Black or Argent lower body panels
Black or Argent hood
Mach 1 side body stripes
Mach 1 deck lid stripe
Brushed aluminum wheel covers and trim rings
Desirable options
4-speed manual or 3-speed automatic transmission
351CJ engine
Power disc brakes
Mach 1 Sports Interior
Front and rear spoilers
14 inch forged aluminum wheels
Air conditioning
Power side windows
Traction Lok differential
Fold-down rear seat

This convertible has the Decor Group, tape stripes, Tu-Tone hood and rear deck spoiler.

104

Chapter 9

1974-78 Mustang IIs

★	1974-78 Hardtop
★	1974-78 Fastback
★★	1975-78 Mach 1 with V-8
★★★	1976-78 Cobra II with V-8
★★★	1978 King Cobra

1974

Ford had high hopes for the Mustang II. The company envisioned that the redesigned 1974 Mustang II would repeat the fantastic success of the original. Market research had shown that youthful buyers, who at one time came in droves to buy Mustangs, were now buying cars like the Maverick and Plymouth Duster, while those interested in more performance opted for the Datsun 240Z and a host of other imports. All these cars had one thing in common: they were a lot smaller than the first-generation Mustang.

Although the Mustang II was a completely different Mustang, the Mustang II incorporated many of the original's styling cues. Most obvious was the front grille and the side sculpturing. During its five years of production, the Mustang II's basic styling on its two bodies, the hardtop and the fastback, did not change. Ford made no convertibles.

The Mustang II was no longer a pony car; it now was classified as a subcompact and as

Of the two Mustang II body styles, the notchback has less potential collector value. This 1975 Ghia got the Silver Luxury Group, which included silver paint, vinyl half-roof, hood ornament, opera windows and a crushed cranberry red velour interior. This sort of Mustang was a far cry from the original's simplicity. *Ford Motor Company*

105

The fastback Mustang IIs were more interesting. This 1974 Mach 1 was basically all-show and no-go, as the top engine option was a 109 hp V-6. Those built during 1975-78 could be had with the 302 V-8. *Ford Motor Company*

such, abandoned that market segment to GM's Camaro and Firebird. By 1977, we would see the Camaro outselling the Mustang II. The Mustang II competed with cars like GM's Skyhawk, Starfire and Monza—you remember them, don't you? Overall, the Mustang II did not prove to be the success Ford hoped for. Although sales in its first

In 1976, Ford gave us the Stallion, a black-out trim option. *Ford Motor Company*

More interesting is the 1976 Cobra II. This example has aftermarket wheels. *Joy Jacobs*

There is no shortage of stripes, scoops and spoilers on the Cobra II. *Joy Jacobs*

The year 1978 brought a revision of the Cobra II. Cobra graphics are really blatant. *Ford Motor Company*

year were quite respectable, 385,993 units, the first OPEC oil embargo was primarily the cause: any car that looked small was snapped up by a frantic public.

Although the Mustang II shared the front engine, rear-wheel-drive configuration of the first-generation Mustang, in many ways it was quite different. The front suspension was redesigned and the front springs were now located between the control arms rather than above the upper A-arm, which improved ride quality. Another major differ-

The hood scoop on the 1978 Cobra II faces backwards. *Ford Motor Company*

The Mach 1 Mustang II didn't change much over its five-year production span. This is a 1978. *Gary Baum*

ence was the use of a front subframe designed to isolate the engine from the rest of the chassis. This was necessary because the Mustang II's standard four-cylinder engine vibrated quite a bit. Other improvements included the use of rack-and-pinion steering, standard front disc brakes, staggered shock rear suspension and a standard four-speed manual transmission.

The standard engine throughout the Mustang II's production was a 2300 cc (140 ci) inline four-cylinder engine. Even though

The T-Top roof option makes this Mach 1 rarer. *Gary Baum*

Mustang II's interior was fairly well laid out. Seats didn't offer much lateral support. This is from a 1978 Mach 1. *Gary Baum*

it sported features such as a single overhead cam and a crossflow cylinder head with canted valves, it pumped out a meager 88 hp—clearly not enough for a car approaching 3,000 pounds. The optional engine for the 1974 model year was a German-built 2.8 liter V-6 (171 ci). A good little engine, its 105 hp was again not enough for the Mustang II. In fact, when the car first came out, it was panned by the automotive press for being too slow.

The Ghia took the place of the Grande as the luxury Mustang II. Ford acquired the Italian Ghia design studios in 1970, and to lend an exotic, European flavor, the Ghia badge was used on the car. Ghia did contribute to the initial design but the Ghia Mustang itself was pure Detroit.

If you wanted performance, or at least the looks of performance, the Mach 1 was available on the fastback body. The fastback, by the way, had become a hatchback.

Following the Mustang tradition, the option list was as long as ever, particularly with creature comforts. A nice feature was the use of a more informative dash: a tachometer and fuel and temperature gauges were

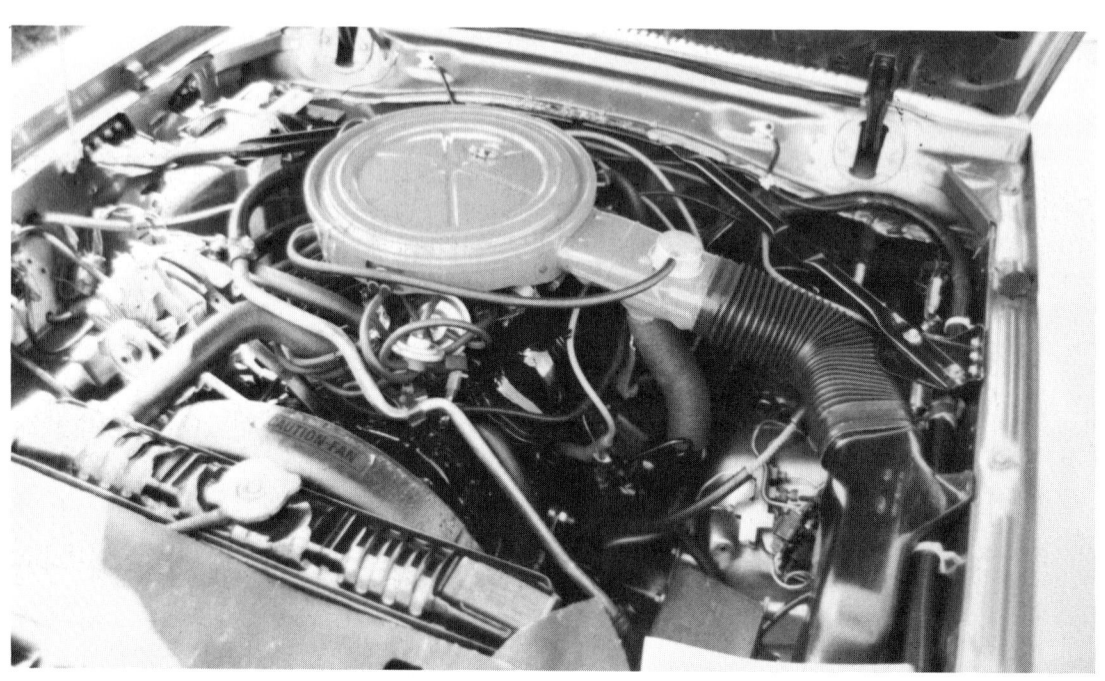

The German-built V-6 was an excellent engine; however the Mustang II was a bit too heavy for it.

With the 302, the Mustang II could give decent street performance.

standard. Unfortunately, seats with a reclining adjustment were still years away.

1975-76

The year 1975 saw few changes. The Ghia got an opera window, the rage of the mid-seventies luxury set. More significant was the availability of the 302 V-8. Even though it was available with an automatic transmission and rated at only 140 hp, this engine was a giant step forward. Typical 0-60 mph times were in the ten-second range and quarter-mile times in the seventeen-second range. Even *Road & Track,* which traditionally pans American-made cars, grudgingly admitted that the V-8 Mach 1 wasn't a bad car.

More important, at least from an image point of view, was the introduction of the Cobra II in 1976. This was a cosmetic package available on the fastback body. Ford offered three colors: white with blue stripes,

With the usual hot-rod modifications, the Mustang II could really perform. This one has been modified with headers, high-rise intake manifold, and Holley carburetor. The Cobra valve covers and chrome air cleaner added some underhood class.

The ultimate Mustang II, at least visually, was the 1978 King Cobra. *Dale Rabe*

The King Cobra's hood was dominated by this decal.

No part of the King Cobra escaped the stylists hand. Note striping on bumper and rear window moldings.

blue with white stripes and black with gold, the last choice emulating the Shelby Hertz cars. The Cobra II consisted of front and rear spoilers, simulated hood scoop, rear side window louvers, rocker panel stripes, aluminum wheels with RWL tires and color-keyed mirrors. Cobra snake decals were affixed on each front fender, while a Cobra emblem was placed in the center of the blacked-out grille.

The Cobra II's standard engine was the four-cylinder with the V-6, and the 302 V-8 was optional. Naturally, only the V-8 Cobra IIs should be considered by collectors. The use of the Cobra name infuriated Shelby Mustang owners and enthusiasts. The Cobra name always invoked images of tremendous power and performance, and it was felt that the Cobra II just didn't live up to the name. This may be true, but Ford owned the rights to the name, and that name helped to improve the Mustang's image and increase sales.

Another cosmetic package was available in 1976 as the Stallion model, which coincided with similar offerings from Ford's Maverick and Pinto.

1977-78

Only minor styling changes came in 1977. The Ghia could be had with the Ghia Sports

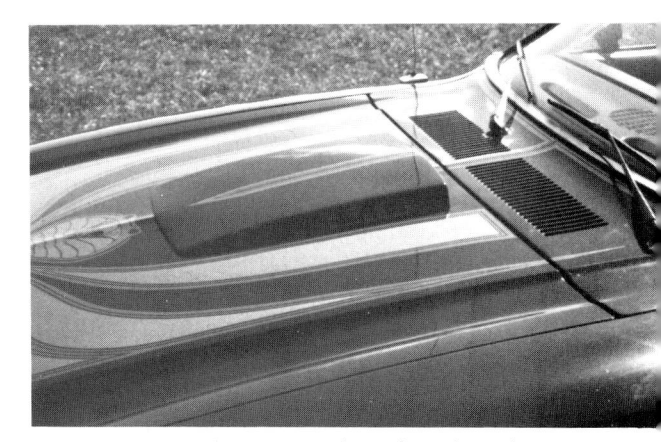

The scoop was the same unit as found on the Cobra II. Still non-functional, engine size was displayed in liters rather than cubic inches.

113

Group (another cosmetic package), and notchbacks could be ordered with a pop-up sunroof. Fastbacks were available with a T-top, while the Cobra II was now available in additional color schemes, white with red and white with green. The Sports Performance Package finally added the four-speed manual transmission to the 302 V-8, transforming the Mustang into a decent performer by seventies standards.

Mustang II sales by 1977 were in decline, and for the first time, the Camaro outsold Mustang.

The year 1978 was the last for the Mustang II, by this time a tired design. The Cobra II got new garish side stripes, but the new rear window louver, similiar to the Boss 302's Sports Slats, was attractive.

King Cobra

The last cosmetic permutation of the Mustang II was the King Cobra, which borrowed several features from Pontiac's Firebird Trans Am. A large snake decal graced the hood, which also had a rear-facing hood scoop, nonfunctional of course. Rather than use the Cobra II's front spoiler, the King Cobra came with a front air dam. Another unique feature was the rear wheelwell spoilers, again borrowed from Pontiac.

The King Cobra came with the 302 engine, four-speed transmission, power brakes, power steering (variable-ratio) and wire style aluminum wheels, as well as the Rallye package that provided heavy-duty springs, adjustable shocks, and a rear sway bar. The T-top was optional.

Prospects

From a collector's viewpoint, the 1974 offers little. These cars, simply because they were so underpowered, just weren't that much fun to drive. Handling and braking

A nice touch on this King Cobra is the T-top roof.

The ultimate Mustang II was the Kemp-Cobra race car. Powered by a modified 351C, it was very fast, but unreliable.

were actually pretty good, but with no power, you couldn't take advantage of it.

If you have your heart set on a second-generation Mustang, the King Cobra is the most interesting, followed by the V-8 Cobra IIs and Mach 1s. You aren't going to see much appreciation in these cars, but on the other hand, your best bet is to get one now. Parts unique to these cars aren't being reproduced, so it is much more of a challenge to restore one.

Even though second-generation Mustangs aren't highly regarded, they do have a decent following, and you do see more and more of these cars at shows. The trouble is that they are constantly being compared to the first-generation Mustangs, which is natural, but which isn't really fair. If you compare the second-generation to other mid- to late-1970s offerings, you'll find that the Mustang II is a superior car and a good performer.

1974–78 Mustang
Base engine*
Type: OHV inline 4 cyl.
Bore x stroke, in.: 3.78×3.13
Displacement, ci: 140
Compression ratio: 8.4:1
Horsepower: 88@5000 rpm
Torque, lb.-ft.: 116@2600 rpm
Chassis and drivetrain
Transmission: 4-speed manual
Optional Transmissions: 3-speed automatic
Front suspension: Independent, coil springs, tube shocks
Rear suspension: Live axle, leaf springs, tube shocks
Axle ratio: 3.08:1
Brakes: Disc/drum
Steering: Rack-and-pinion
General
Wheelbase, In.: 96.2
Height, in.: 49.9
Width, in.: 70.2
Length, in.: 175.0
Track, front/rear, in.: 55.5/55.6
Curb weight, lb.: 2,679
*1974

Chapter 10

1979-89 Mustangs

★✶	1979-89 Two-door
★★	1979-89 Three-door
★★★	1983-89 Convertible
★★★★★	1979½ Pace Car
★★★★	1984 20th Anniversary Edition three-door
★★★★★	1984 20th Anniversary Edition convertible
★★★★	1984-85 SVO
★★★	1982-84 GT
★★★✶	1985-89 GT
★★★★	1983-89 GT convertible
★★★★★	1981 McLaren Mustang
★★★★★	1985-89 Saleen Mustang

1979

The third-generation Mustang was a total departure from the Mustang II. No attempt was made to connect it with past Mustangs in terms of styling, but proportionally, it still had the long-hood, short-deck styling theme that began with first-generation Mustangs. Initially, the third-generation Mustang was available as a two-door sedan and three-door fastback, with the convertible becoming available in the 1983 model year.

In terms of size, this Mustang was larger than the Mustang II. Wheelbase increased to 100.4 inches; it lengthened four inches; it stood on a wider track, yet it was lighter. Reflecting the importance of aerodynamics, its Coefficient of Drag (CD) was twenty-five percent less than the Mustang II's at 0.44 (0.46 for the sedan), a good figure for 1979 standards. Speaking of CD figures, a baseball has a CD of 0.45, a bullet 0.25 and a 747 jet airliner 0.02. As we shall see, improved aerodynamics are part of the reason

1979 Mustang two-door. Except for nose and rear treatments, the third generation body has remained essentially the same during its ten years of production. *Ford Motor Company*

116

The 1979 Pace Car with its unique graphics and body work. Most owners chose not to apply the side lettering, although you will more often see the horses. *Ford Motor Company*

The 1982 Mustang GT brought performance back to Ford. This 1982 GT has the TRX suspension package, part of which included these attractive wheels. T-top was an option from 1982–87, although there are some 1988s equipped with it as well. The rear side windows were owner tinted.

The 1982 GT came with a front air dam and a large, non-functional hood scoop reminiscent of late 1960s Mustangs.

for the current Mustang GT's top speed, which approaches 150 mph.

The new Mustang's styling was thoroughly modern—in fact, its sloped nose has been widely copied. Even though the third-generation Mustang's styling received mostly minor yearly updates, it was still based on the same body shell and platform as the second generation. The most significant change occurred with the 1987 models, which incorporated Ford's aero look, but the Mustang still was essentially the same car it was in 1979. Even though it was considered a somewhat dated design by 1989, the Mustang sure had staying power, which can be seen in the production figures.

Like first- and second-generation Mustangs which were based on other Ford products, the Mustang this time around used the Fairmont platform, but bore no resemblance to the boxy Fairmont sedan. The front suspension used McPherson struts to replace the conventional upper A-arms. The coil spring was located on the lower arm and on the chassis. This type of suspension was

T-top on this 1982 GT provided open-air ambiance without the drawbacks of a true convertible. This one has an owner-installed steering wheel.

The 1984 styling changes were minimal from those made in 1983.

A 1984 20th Anniversary Special.

Although this 1984 20th Anniversary Special and all 1984 GTs sported twin outlet exhausts, the Mustang would not come with a true dual exhaust system until 1985.

found on most imported cars and had the advantage of being cheaper to manufacture. The rear suspension used coil springs with four bar links to locate the rear axle. A front sway bar was standard, while V-8 Mustangs and those equipped with the optional handling suspension also came with a rear sway bar.

Ford exerted a great effort to make the 1979 Mustang a handling car. The Mustang was available optionally with the Michelin 190/65R 390 TRX tires, which in 1979 were considered state of the art. These 65 series tires could only be mounted on a special size wheel rim, measuring 15.4 by 5.9 inches. When combined with specially calibrated sway bars, shocks and springs, the Mustang did indeed handle. The TRX tires were available until 1984.

Four engines were available on the 1979 Mustang. The standard engine was the same 2.3 liter four-cylinder that also came with the Mustang II, pumping out a paltry 88 hp. The 2.8 liter V-6 was optional. The performance engines were a turbocharged 2.3 liter four-cylinder and the familiar 302 V-8 5.0 liter in two-barrel trim. By this time, engine size was generally referred to in metric terms, liters versus cubic inches.

Special identification on the 20th included side stripes and original Mustang emblems. Mud flaps were owner-installed. *Steven and Joy Jacobs*

Ford made much hoopla about the turbocharged four-cylinder; basically this engine was an attempt to combine the high mileage characteristics of a small engine with the high horsepower of a V-8. Rated at 132 hp, only eight horsepower less than the 302, it proved to be a dud. Although Ford did strengthen the engine internally, it had a high failure rate. Turbo technology since 1979 has come a long way, but most turbocharged engines still suffer from turbo lag and do require special maintenance. The turbo four-cylinder was standard equipment on the third-generation Cobra Mustang, available only as a fastback.

Included on the Cobra were the TRX suspension package and appropriate identification. A large snake hood decal was, thankfully, an option.

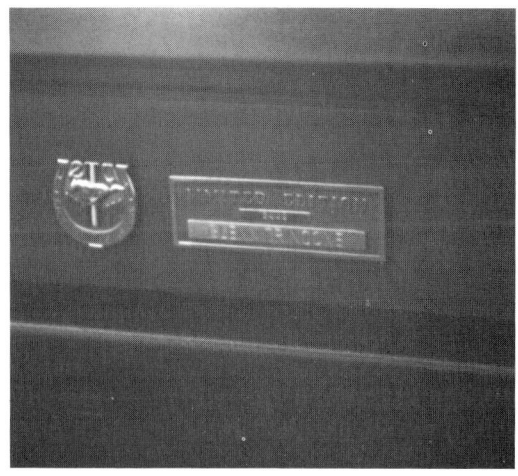

These two plaques on the passenger side of the dash identified the 20th as such. To collectors, these are important for originality's sake.

The 20th used a special steering wheel. Later, the Mustang SVO would use the same unit. *Steven Jacobs*

The four-barrel 302 powered most of the 20th Anniversary Specials. *Steven Jacobs*

The Turbo GT four-cylinder never really caught on. It was hard to compete with the low-end torque and response of a V-8.

More reliable was the optional 302 V-8 engine. In two-barrel, single-exhaust form, it was rated at 140 hp. Even at this low output, the 302 V-8 was a bit too much for the rear suspension—severe axle hop and tramp were evident under drag starts.

The high point for 1979 was the Mustang Pace Car. The Mustang was chosen to pace the 1979 Indianapolis 500 race. The actual Pace Cars used in the race had specially modified 302s, whereas the street Pace Cars could be had with the 302 or the turbo four. About 11,000 of these were built; all had the same pewter and black paint treatment highlighted with orange and red tape stripes. Pace Car lettering decals were dealer- or customer-installed.

Other features of the Pace Car were a rear spoiler, front air dam with integral foglamps, pop-up sunroof, and rear-facing nonfunc-

Rarest 1984 is the 20th Anniversary Special convertible.

Rear styling definitely has a Mercedes influence.

The 1985 Mustangs were restyled. Nose resembles the SVO's.

Besides the front restyle, the 1985 Mustang was still basically unchanged from the 1979.

tional hood scoop. Inside, this Mustang came with Recaro seats.

During the year, the 2.8 liter German-built V-6 was replaced with the now old 200 ci inline six.

Along with the performance Cobra, the luxury Mustangs were the Ghia models, available in either two- or three-door form.

1980-81

The years 1980-81 were a low point for the Mustang, at least from a performance point of view. The 302 engine was dropped from the option list and replaced by a 255 ci version, rated at 119 hp. The decrease in displacement was reached by reducing the bore from 4.00 to 3.68 inches. Although the 255 engine looked the same as the 302, it used considerably lightened internal parts and block, so it is not recommended that it be modified for more power. The 255 was available only with the automatic transmission.

During 1985-86, this 15×7 inch aluminum wheel with Goodyear tires replaced the TRX wheel.

Other engines included the 200 in. six-cylinder and the 2.3 liter four-cylinder in turbocharged and non-turbocharged forms.

Ford's foray into producing a Europeanized Mustang was the 1984½ SVO. In spite of many technical innovations, it found little acceptance among the typical Mustang enthusiast due to high cost, while it lacked the true sophistication and refinement of a European sports sedan to appeal to that market.

Sixteen inch wheels were part of the SVO.

Specials

The Cobra now sported the Pace Car's front air dam, hood scoop and rear spoiler. The comfortable Recaro seats were optional.

The same engine lineup was carried over for 1981, save for the deletion of the turbo four-cylinder.

McLaren Mustang

The turbo four, however, was part of the McLaren Mustang. This was a special run of 249 McLaren-modified Mustangs that featured extensive body and interior modifications. Significant hand workmanship went into these cars, and like the Saleen Mustangs, these McLaren Mustangs were available through the Ford dealer network. Expensive at about $25,000 a copy, it was hard to justify such a high cost for a Mustang that really handled well but could only do the quarter-mile in about seventeen seconds or so. However, the McLaren Mustang was a precursor of the performance to be delivered by the Ford Motor Company's cars.

1982–85

Things heated up a bit in 1982: the Mustang GT was reintroduced after a twelve-

The familiar 2.3 liter four-cylinder was highly modified for use in the SVO. It pumped out 175 hp on the 1984½ version and 205 on the 1985½.

This 1987 GT has the rare T-top option.

The 1987 Mustang GT got new aluminum wheels, aero-look side skirts and an impressive rear wing.

year hiatus. Standard engine was the 302 V-8, sporting a somewhat larger two-barrel carburetor, aluminum intake manifold and a slightly better single exhaust system. Because the engine was rated at 157 hp, it was necessary for Ford to install rear traction bars to help control rear wheel hop. The GT also featured the front air dam, rear spoiler and front-facing simulated hood scoop. The handsome TRX wheels and tires were also standard.

In 1982, Ford first offered the optional T-top roof. It looks nice, but be forewarned that it may leak.

The 302 was available also on all other Mustang models, which included the L, GL and GLX (the Ghia nameplate had been dropped).

This was also the year the-third generation Camaro and Firebird were introduced. There is no question that GM's restyled pony cars were attractive and boasted excellent performance to boot. Since then, the Mustang/Camaro rivalry has helped to push performance to levels equaling late sixties Mustang acceleration, while surpassing the earlier cars in ride, handling and braking. While styling is subjective and performance about equal, the Mustang GT since 1982 has emerged clearly the winner when it comes to cost—and it has been judged to be more fun to drive. I like the generous use of glass in the Mustang which gives the car a more open interior. While The Camaro's sloped windshield may make the car attractive, it is difficult to see out.

In 1983, additional development and progress arrived. The Mustang front end was restyled, while the rear got European-looking taillamps. A third body style joined the line-up, an eye-catching convertible. The convertible was also available as a GT, sport-

In 1987, after eight years, Ford finally gave the Mustang a new interior.

ing all the GT features: TRX wheels, graphics and, of course, the 302 V-8 engine.

The 302 was uprated to 175 hp by the use of a Holley 600 cfm four-barrel carburetor. Wheel hop was still a problem, even though the 1983 GT came with traction bars (as did the 1982 GTs).

Momentum did not stop with the 1984 Mustangs. In fact, the Mustang was quickly becoming a serious performance car. The Mustang GT continued sporting the 175 hp version of the 302 HO, but only with the five-speed manual transmission. Factory literature also listed a 205 hp version with dual exhausts, but this particular engine never appeared that year. Mustang GTs with the automatic transmission got an EFI 302 HO rated at 165 hp.

Specials

Ford also produced the Turbo GT Mustang. This particular version came with a much-improved turbocharged 2.3 liter four-cylinder engine. Electronic fuel injection raised horsepower output to 145, and this time around, the turbo four was reliable. However, it could not compare with the raw torque of the 302 HO.

SVO

The model that could compare with the Mustang GT was the limited-edition Mustang SVO. SVO stands for Special Vehicle Operations, which is the performance arm of Ford Motor Company. The SVO was a sophisticated Mustang designed to combine handling, acceleration and fuel economy, while appealing to a more sophisticated buyer.

The heart of the SVO was yet another version of the 2.3 liter four-cylinder engine. Similar to the Turbo GT engine, the SVO's four-cylinder came with an intercooler and tuned port fuel injection system that boosted horsepower to 175. Everything on the en-

Interior space remained unchanged. Fold-down seats, standard on all hatchbacks, increased cargo volume. The pouch on this 1987 GT stores the T-top panels.

T-tops were still available in 1987.

The 1987-89 GTs came with this aluminum turbine wheel.

gine was electronically controlled, including the turbocharger. Maximum boost was 14 psi. The SVO came only with a five-speed manual.

Other features of the SVO included a revised front suspension with Koni adjustable shocks, four-wheel disc brakes and Quadra-Shock rear suspension designed to cure the Mustang's wheel hop tendencies. The SVO also used 16×7 inch aluminum wheels with P225/50VR Goodyear NCT tires.

Driver comfort wasn't neglected either. The SVO came with highly adjustable bucket seats, special leather-wrapped steering wheel, dead pedal for the driver's left foot and a premium stereo system. It was a fairly well furnished car in standard form.

The only major options were air conditioning, power windows and locks, cassette radio, pop-up sun roof and leather interior.

The SVO was available only in black, charcoal, silver or red, all with a charcoal interior.

Externally, the SVO could be distinguished by its unique grille, hood scoop, wheel spats in front of the rear wheelwell openings and biplane rear spoiler.

The 1986 edition of the SVO sported some relatively minor engine improvements which boosted horsepower to 205. The suspension was stiffened and steering ratio reduced for quicker response. The car was a better driver; shifter position was changed while shift and clutch throws were reduced. Like the 1985 Mustang GT, the SVO came with unidirectional Goodyear P225/60VR-15 Eagle tires.

In spite of the SVO's relative sophistication when compared to the Mustang GT, it failed to sell in great enough numbers. Yes, it did handle better than the GT and it was almost as quick, but the SVO cost about $4,000 more at $16,000, putting the SVO Mustang in a different class altogether. For me, the SVO lacked the visceral excitement of the Mustang GT's 302 and its instantaneous response. Once the SVO got going, you realized that it definitely had the power. The lesson for Ford was: If you're going to compete with European highline performance cars, you'll need a better platform than the Mustang.

Nevertheless, you can expect the Mustang SVO to become a collectible. It still is the most technically sophisticated Mustang ever built, and it was built in limited numbers. The 1986 version is preferable.

20th Anniversary Special

One instant collectible that appeared in 1984 was the 20th Anniversary Edition Mustang. These were all Mustang GTs, three-door coupes and convertibles, painted Oxford White (Code 9L) with Canyon Red interiors. Engine choice was either the 302 HO or the Turbo GT four-cylinder. The 20th also came with the articulated sports seats, the same as the SVO's, but without the adjustable lumbar support. The rest of the package included a special lower panel tape treatment with GT350 letters and numerals (let's upset those Shelby owners again!), original Mustang fender emblems

The 1986 and later performance 302 HOs came with fuel injection.

The standard engine for the third generation Mustang was this lackluster 2.3 liter four-cylinder.

and the two 20th Anniversary Dash Panel badges.

The first of the anniversary badges was a horseshoe medallion located on the dash. These were not installed at the time of manufacture; rather, each was shipped separately to the dealership to be installed in the cars. As only one badge per car was made, many have been lost or were never installed in the cars at all.

Three to four months after purchase, the owner was sent a form to fill out so that the second medallion could be obtained. This was the serial number owner's plaque. It read "Limited Edition" followed by a serial number (unrelated to the VIN) and below that the owner's name.

Unfortunately, the only way you can tell a 20th Anniversary Edition from other Mustangs is by these two medallions, as all the other features of the 20th Anniversary package can easily be duplicated. The two medallions and original window sticker are needed to establish the authenticity of such a car. In addition, all 20th Anniversary Mustangs were built in March 1984.

As can be seen from the production figures, the convertibles are fewest in number.

Optional from 1983-86 on was the aluminum head 3.8 liter V-6.

Mustangs haven't seen so much race action since the 1960s. This is Gary Smith's car at the 1987 Pikes Peak. *Paul McLaughlin*

And I would give preference to those powered by the 302, even though fewer were built with the turbo four.

1985-86

The 1985-86 Mustangs got another minor restyle. This time, the grille opening re-

Awesome road-racing machines were the Roush Racing Mustangs. This one was driven by Scott Pruett. *Paul McLaughlin*

sembled the SVO's. The big news, however, was in the engine compartment. Still sporting a Holley 600 cfm four-barrel, the 302 now came with stainless steel tube headers, a camshaft that used roller lifters and a true dual exhaust system. Horsepower jumped to 210 hp at 4600 rpm and torque to 265 lb-ft at 3400 rpm. Mustangs with the automatic transmission came with the 165 hp version of the 302 HO. To control wheel hop, the GT came with the Quadra-Shock rear suspension. Handling improved with the replacement of the TRX wheels and tires by Goodyear Eagle P225/60VR15 tires on 15×7 aluminum wheels. The Mustang was definitely improving with age.

For 1986, the Mustang remained essentially the same, although horsepower dropped to 200, and the Holley four-barrel was replaced by sequential multiport fuel injection.

1987-89

The Mustang's current incarnation began in 1987, receiving the most extensive restyle since 1979—and finally, a new interior. The new styling was more compatible with Ford's aerodynamic look. The GT also came with a revised air dam, side skirts and a new rear spoiler. Although tires remained the same, the 1987-89 GTs came with a new aluminum turbine wheel. If all that flash proved too much, beginning in 1987, you could get the GT engine and suspension in the LX Mustang, whether it was a two- or three-door.

Ford engineers squeezed an additional 25 hp and 35 lb-ft of torque from the 302, reaching 225 hp at 4400 rpm with 300 lb-ft torque at 3000 rpm. This was achieved by using truck cylinder heads, larger fuel injectors, higher flow intake runners and larger throttle body. Mustangs with the automatic transmission were rated five horsepower less.

With the extra power, acceleration was a little better, mid-fourteens in the quarter-mile, but top speed approached 150 mph. You may ask yourself: How can a 225 hp Mustang GT outrun a first-generation high-performance Mustang, such as the Boss 351? The 1987-89 Mustangs are lighter and owe their top speed to a low numerical rear axle ratio. The older Mustangs needed a lot of gear to get their extra bulk moving, and the youngest Mustangs have much better aerodynamics.

However, it is a pointless exercise to compare the first generation Mustangs with the

It's OK again to modify your Mustang. This one has been decked out by Kamei, and the wheels are Jongbloed modular wheels. *Kamei USA Auto Extras*

Saleen Mustangs had the advantage of factory backing. This was the third 1985 convertible built. *Paul McLaughlin*

If the street racer look of the Mustang GT was not your cup of tea, you could get the exact same engine and suspension on the LX Mustang. This is a 1987 LX convertible. *Ford Motor Company*

third generation. They both have their positive points and their loyal followings.

Specials
Saleen Mustang

Mention should be made of the distinctive Saleen Mustangs, which first appeared in 1985. These are Mustangs that have been modified by Saleen Autosport Incorporated, much in the way that Carroll Shelby modified Mustangs back in the 1960s. The modifications are primarily of the suspension and bodywork, as well as the interior. By maintaining strict quality control, Saleen Mustangs can be purchased through the Ford dealer network. Like the Shelby Mustangs, the Saleen Mustangs have special identification plates. Kits are also available, so that the enthusiast can modify his or her Mustang to match budget and taste. Whether the Saleen Mustangs will reach the same high level of collectability as the Shelby Mustangs remains to be seen.

Prospects

Besides the 1979 Pace Cars, the 20th Anniversary Special and the SVO, GT convertibles should be regarded as collectibles in the making. The 1985 and later versions with their distinctive styling and high horsepower demonstrate a higher propensity for appreciation. These Mustangs will be considered used cars for some time to come as they still haven't bottomed out yet.

Regarding other four- and six-cylinder Mustangs, it is unlikely that they'll ever have any collector value.

The star ratings in this chapter reflect future potential value—not current value because most third-generation Mustangs are still declining in value as of 1989.

1979–89 Mustang
Base engine*
Type: OHV inline 4 cyl.
Bore x stroke, in.: 3.78×3.13
Displacement, ci: 140
Compression ratio: 9.0:1
Horsepower: 88@4400 rpm
Torque, lb.-ft.: 118@2800 rpm
Chassis and drivetrain
Transmission: 4-speed manual
Optional Transmissions: 5-speed manual, 3-speed, 4-speed automatics
Front suspension: Independent, coil springs, tube shocks
Rear suspension: Live axle, coil springs, tube shocks
Axle ratio: 3.08:1
Brakes: Disc/drum
Steering: Rack-and-pinion
General
Wheelbase, in.: 100.4
Height, in.: 51.5
Width, in.: 69.1
Length, in.: 179.1
Track, front/rear, in.: 56.6/57.0
Curb weight, lb.: 2,516
*1979

Chapter 11

1990-93 Mustangs

★✓	1990-93 Two-Door LX
★★	1990-93 Three-Door LX
★★★	1990-93 Convertible
★★★★	1990-93 GT Convertible
★★★★✓	1993 Mustang Cobra
★★★★★	1993 Mustang Cobra R
Add ✓	1990-93 LX 5.0L Sport

1990
Like the previous year, there wasn't much to distinguish the 1990 Mustang. The body was the same; in the interior, the most discernible change was the addition of a driver's-side airbag. Less obvious, but a feature that had been due for a long time, was the use of a 140mph speedometer on the GT and 5.0L equipped LX models. The 2.3L Mustang still used a unit that stopped at 85mph.

Introduced in 1989, the 5.0L LX models gained popularity in 1990 for several rea-

As with previous collectible Mustangs, look for the high performance convertibles for the most collectible potential. These are still depreciating and it will be a few years yet before they bottom out. This is a 1992 Mustang GT convertible. *Ford Motor Co.*

137

The 1993 Mustang Cobra stands out as a high point among third generation performance Mustangs. It gave the enthusiast high performance in a Mustang that was easier to live with on a day-to-day basis. *Ford Motor Co.*

sons. Without all the aero effects, the Mustang looked a bit cleaner and therefore attracted less attention. It was also less expensive, and the 5.0L LX sedan was lighter, too. This was ideal for the performance enthusiast because the lighter body shell made for a faster Mustang. The 5.0L LX's shared the same drivetrain and suspension componentry as the GTs.

You'd think that with 1990 being the 25th year that the Mustang was in production, Ford would have released a special model to commemorate this event. This was not to be. The closest Ford got to was the 5.0L LX Convertible Special—all painted Deep Emerald Green with a white leather interior and top. These cars were limited to a special production run of only 4,600.

1991-1993

The biggest change for 1991 was the use of five-spoke 16x7in cast aluminum wheels on the Mustang GT and 5.0L LX. Otherwise, it was the same old Mustang. In fact, the 1991 and 1992 Mustang brochures use most of the same photography.

1993 Ford Mustang Cobra

In 1993, Ford released another special Mustang, the Cobra. The 1993 Mustang Cobra was more or less a stopgap measure until the redesigned fourth generation Mustang debuted with the 1994 model year. There wasn't much that Ford could do to counter the redesigned 1993 Camaro/Firebird. The Cobra name still carried a wallop. Unlike the previous Cobra II and 1979-81 Cobra option packages, the 1993 incarnation of the Cobra had some bite to it. Starting with the 5.0L GT hatchback, the Cobra got a more sedate side skirt treatment, redesigned rear wing spoiler, and appropriate Cobra badges on the front fenders and grille. The engines was modified with the previously available, over-the-counter-only GT-40 cylinder heads and intake which resulted in better breathing. Along with a recalibrated engine computer and other components, the 5.0L V-8 was rated at 235hp. This wasn't much over the 5.0L V-8 which was rated at 205hp.

The big difference was in the suspension. Instead of using the suspension from the Mustang GT, the Cobra used the base 2.3Ls

The Saleen Mustang certainly has made a name for itself and it is the most recognizable Mustang Special. The Saleen name is synonymous with performance. As of this writing, Saleen is back in business, building a limited number of Mustangs for the discerning Mustang enthusiast.

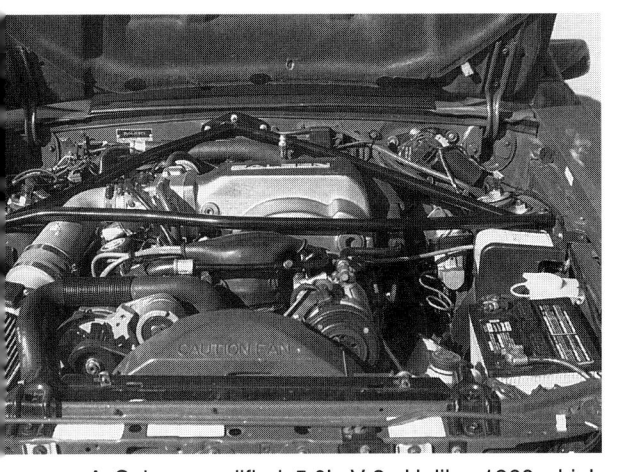

Saleen convertibles are particularly attractive. Low profile tires, shorter springs, and a modified aerodynamic package give the Saleen Mustang its understated yet serious look.

A Saleen-modified 5.0L V-8. Unlike 1960s high performance engines, most aftermarket engines today idle just like the stock engine, yet put out more horsepower. Modern electronics and fuel injection are a big help in smoothing things out.

rear springs and front strut cartridges. The rear sway bar was smaller as well. The use of larger 17in diameter wheels with 245/45ZR Goodyear tires was to give the Cobra equal, if not better cornering and handling than a stock GT.

The result was a softer riding Mustang with a little more acceleration than the GT in a unique package. Personally, I found the suspension too soft, especially at high speeds.

A total of 5,000 Cobra Mustangs were built.

1993 Ford Mustang Cobra R

In addition to the 1993 Cobras, Ford's SVT Division built a small run of 107 Cobra R Mustangs designed for use in showroom-stock racing. While mechanically similar to the standard Cobra, Cobra Rs were outfitted with a firmer suspension and were only available in white. Several factors made it difficult for the R model to compete against GM's redesigned 1993 Firebird and Camaro. The Mustang's brakes, while adequate for street use, weren't up to the task on the track. In addition, the Mustang's small gas tank made for more frequent pit stops, and the 5.0L V-8 just didn't put out enough power. These problems were all addressed later on the 1995 version of the Cobra R.

However, the biggest problem the R model had is that few actually ever made it to the track. Most were bought by collectors rather than racers—which was not what Ford had intended.

The Steeda GT comes with a 275hp version of the 5.0L engine along with a host of suspension and interior modification. The engine is EPA legal. *Steeda*

Specials

Like the special Shelby Mustangs produced during 1965-70 years, there was a proliferation of high performance aftermarket Mustangs available for the enthusiast. Best known were the Saleen Mustangs, but after Saleen ran into difficulties in the early 1990s, other specials emerged. All these Mustangs have the same things in common—they are Mustangs that have been modified and engineered for better acceleration and handling in a visually distinctive package. Whereas Ford's special, the Cobra, was very much a package that provided a balance between ride and performance, the aftermarket specials put most of their emphasis on all-out performance.

Whether or not these special Mustangs will appreciate in the same manner as the original Shelby Mustangs remains to be seen.

Steeda GT

The Steeda GT has been built by Steeda Autosports—one of the major aftermarket Mustang performance-parts vendors—since 1990. These were available directly from Steeda or could be conveniently ordered through Ford dealers.

The Steeda's aerodynamic treatment is subtly different from the stock Mustang GT. The rear valence panel is designed to let air through in order to reduce drag. Equally distinctive are the attractive Steeda Five Star wheels.

Not so noticeable are the many suspension improvements made. The stock springs are discarded and replaced with higher-rate springs that reduce roll and ride height. Polyurethane bushings are used wherever possible and a strut tower brace helps tighten up the Mustang's front structure. Improved braking can be provided by an optional four-wheel disc brake system. For the enthusiasts wanting more, additional suspension modifications can be ordered, including sub-frame braces, Tokico cockpit-adjustable struts and shocks, and larger anti-sway bars.

The Steeda could have been outfitted with a variety of interior trim packages

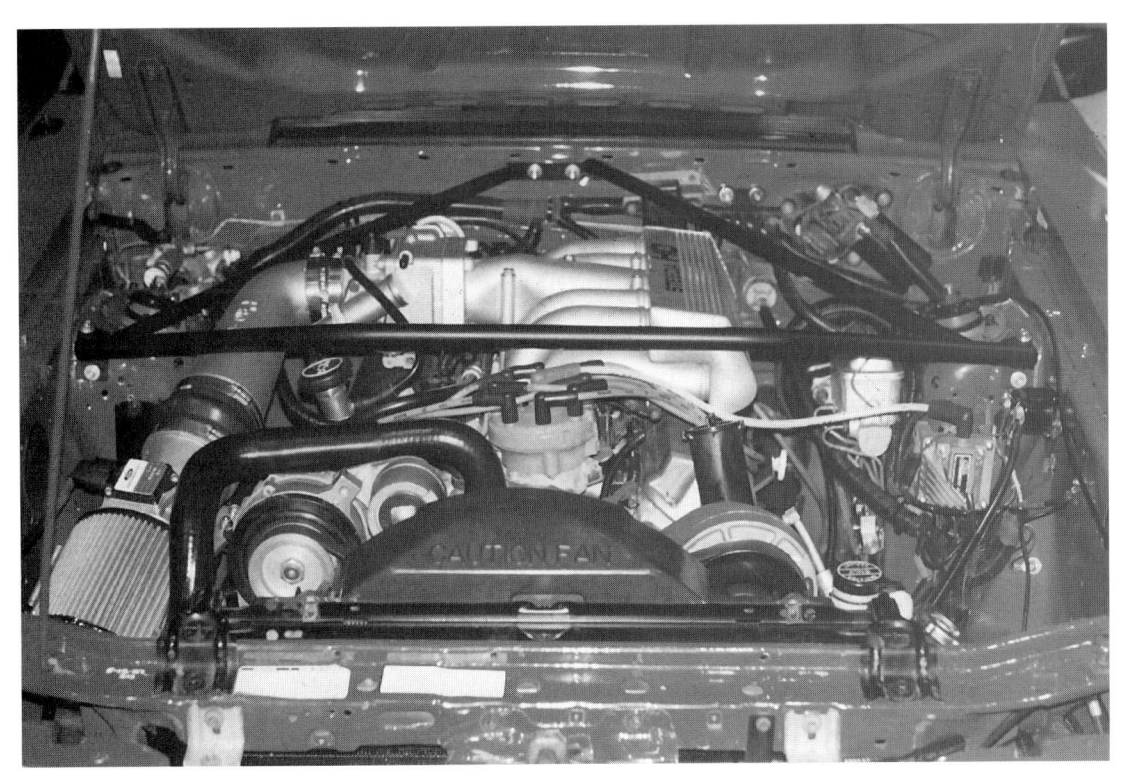

The Steeda's 275hp engine. Note the triangular strut-tower brace which adds some chassis stiffening for better cornering. *Steeda*

including leather and even Flow Fit seats. And as you would expect, the Steeda customer could specify practically any kind of sound system.

The distinctive Steeda GT really shines through in the engine compartment, with the 5.0L engine modified to put out 275 EPA-approved hp. This has been accomplished by a modified fuel-injection system, high-ratio rocker arms, underdrive pulleys, an optimized EEC-IV computer and a freer-flowing exhaust system. The Steeda Mustang will accelerate to 60mph in the mid-five-second range and hit the quarter in the mid-13-second range. Several hundred have been built.

The SAAC MK I, MK II, and SAAC Snake

Affiliated with the Shelby American Automobile Club is the SAAC Car Co.'s series of high performance Mustangs.

There have been three SAAC models—the SAAC MK I, the SAAC MK II, and the SAAC Snake.

The SAAC MK I was built in 1991-92, and was available only to members of the Shelby Automobile Club. All MK Is were based on the three-door Mustang and all were painted white with blue stripes.

The SAAC MK II was the same basic car, but it was also made as a convertible and it was available to the general public—either direct from SAAC or through a select Ford dealer network. In addition to white/blue stripes, the SAAC MK II was available in red/white stripes and black/gold stripes.

The SAAC Snake is basically MK II, but without the specially modified 295hp engine.

The basic 5.0L GT engine of the SAAC MK I & II was modified with technical assistance from Ford's SVO. It was rated at 295hp and was EPA legal. It was equipped with special SVO GT-40 heads and intake mani-

A trio of SAAC MK IIs at Charlotte Speedway. The MK IIs were available to the public. Resemblance to the original Shelby Mustangs is intentional. *SAAC Car Co.*

fold, and a special 2.5in stainless steel dual-exhaust system with low-restriction mufflers. The engine uses the stock GT camshaft and EEC-IV computer.

Considerable work was also done to improve handling. Koni shock absorbers and struts are used with firmer springs that also lower the car's ride height. For additional bracing, a three-point engine compartment brace as used in addition to an interior chassis-stiffening brace. And like the original Shelby Mustangs, the SAAC MK I & II came with a roll bar. Four-wheel five-lug disc brakes are used with semi-metallic linings.

The SAAC comes with distinctive 17x7.5in front and 17x8.5in rear wheels shod with Goodyear P245/50ZR17 Eagle GT tires.

In the interior, all regular Mustang luxury options are standard equipment, such as power windows and locks, air conditioning, and Premium Sound System. The standard interior is finished in leather only.

Performance figures given are similar to the Steeda GT with mid-13-second quarter mile times, a top speed of over 150mph, and handling in the .9G range.

Project Industries Outlaw

The Outlaw XS was built by Kenny Brown's Project Industries and was available as an aftermarket conversion or as a complete car. Kenny Brown is another well-known supplier of aftermarket performance parts and accessories for the Mustang. The Outlaw offers considerable more power than the other Mustang Specials because it comes with a Vortec V-1 supercharged 5.0L V-8 engine. The base engine is rated at 385hp but an optional version rated at 425hp was available.

As you might expect, there is no way that the standard Mustang T5 five-speed transmission can stand up to this kind of torque, so the Outlaw was fitted with either a six-speed manual transmission or a GM 200-4R four-speed automatic.

The suspension benefits from the Kenny Brown MX-17 Advanced Geometry Suspension System include specific springs and a

Beside the stripes and wheels, the SAAC MK I looks stock when compared to a regular production Mustang GT. The engine and suspension have been extensively modified for a healthy boost in performance over the stock Mustang GT. The MK I was sold only to members of the Shelby American Automobile Club.

rear Panhard rod. The chassis is stiffened up with a three-point strut tower brace, a four-point lower chassis brace and an eight-point double cross subframe connectors. SVO five-lug disc brakes are used on all four wheels. Wheels are 17x8.5in with Firestone SX's measuring P275/40ZR17.

The interior was fitted with Recaro SR seats, the Kenny Brown Ultra Street Cage, and Schroth Harness Belts.

Only a handful of these cars have been built so far. Their collectability remains an unknown.

The SAAC Snake offers the same handling as the SAAC MK II but without the MK IIs more powerful 295hp engine. As with the Mk II, the Snake was available as a three door or convertible. *SAAC Car Co.*

The Outlaw XS from Kenny Brown. With a stock 385hp and more available, the XS can obviously accelerate; but with its advanced suspension system, it also handles like a racer. It comes with the Outlaw Power Hood and the Outlaw GT rear wing. *Project Industries*

The roll bars on the SAAC Snake are similar to the type used on 1968-70 Shelby Mustang convertibles. *SAAC Car Co.*

Chapter 12

1994-95 Mustangs

★	Base Mustang
★★	GT Coupe
★★★	GT Convertible
★★★	Cobra Coupe
★★★★	Cobra Convertible
★★★★★	1995 Cobra R 351

Imagine, if you will, if the original 1965 Mustang ran, basically unchanged, for fifteen model years. Would people have continued to buy Mustangs in the same numbers? Probably not, but that was the case during the 1980s. With minimal styling and mechanical changes, Ford was able to continue selling the same car in great enough numbers to

After a fourteen year model run, the third generation Mustang was succeeded by the 1994 model. Completely redesigned in and out, the 1994 Mustang performs better, and still retains the traditional front engine/rear wheel drive layout. The GT shown, is powered by a 215hp version of Ford's 5.0L small-block V-8. *Ford Motor Co.*

Only one other body style complimented the coupe in 1994—a convertible. The standard engine was Ford's 3.8L V-6 rated at 145hp. A removable hardtop was optional on the convertible. Note the side sculpturing which is reminiscent of the original 1965 Mustang. *Ford Motor Co.*

The Interior was redesigned as well on the 1994 Mustang. Dual air bags, a power driver's seat, and tilt-steering are standard equipment. The Coupe features a split-fold back seat. The last time Mustangs got a fold-down rear seat was in 1973. *Ford Motor Co.*

make it profitable and still keep the Mustang mystique going. Alas, all good things must end, and finally, the 1994 Mustang got a much-needed overhaul. Giving Ford a little more impetus to modernize the Mustang was the fact that GM's pony cars, the Camaro and Firebird, were restyled for the 1993 model year.

The most obvious change was in the styling. You may not be able to say that the 1994 Mustang was "all new," but the body (and interior) certainly were. Using the traditional long hood/short deck approach, the 1994 Mustang exhibits the currently fashionable wedge look which tends to make the car look slightly jacked-up sitting still. The side sculpturing definitely evokes the past as

Sharing the same body panels as the Mustang Cobra, the Cobra R is recognizable by its unique hood and wheels. *Ford Motor Co.*

To save weight, the rear seat, air conditioning, and the standard Mustang power accessories were deleted on the Cobra R. *Ford Motor Co.*

does the rear triple-lens taillight treatment, and of course, the Mustang logo.

Whereas the 1979-93 Mustangs were three door hatchbacks, the 1994 became a two-door coupe. Besides the improved styling, getting rid of the hatch resulted in a stiffer, stronger platform. As before, a convertible was available as well.

Beneath its pretty new skin, the Mustang was basically a carryover of the Fox platform. It is definitely more rigid and stiffer—according to Ford the coupe structure is fifty-six percent better in bending stiffness and forty-four percent better in torsion stiffness. It seems that the quest for additional stiffness resulted in a much improved convertible structure as well—sixty-five percent better bending and a noteworthy eighty percent increase in torsional stiffness. This results in a Mustang that is quieter, handles better, and inspires confidence.

Wheelbase is slightly longer (0.75in), while track is 3.7in longer on the base model and 1.9in on the GT. Four-wheel disc brakes are standard with ABS optional.

The suspension, which features minor tweaks, is also carryover—McPherson struts in the front with a live axle in the rear. The quad rear shock arrangement is standard on the GT. One new improvement is the use of a rear anti-sway bar on the base Mustang. Standard on the GT are P205/65R15s with 16x7.5in wheels. with wheels optional. The optional tires are P245/45ZR17s with 17x8in wheels.

Thankfully, the 2.3L four-cylinder engine

was dropped on the 1994 and replaced by the 3.8L V-6 as the standard Mustang engine. The V-6 was last used in a Mustang in 1986. Unlike the 1986 version, the new V-6 has a tuned port injection system and tubular headers which help account for its 145hp output.

For the enthusiast, the tried-and-true 5.0L V-8 is the only one available for the GT. A nice motor, but its 215hp isn't quite enough, at least when compared to the Camaro Z28 or Firebird Trans Am which have 275hp on tap. As expected, Ford's 4.6L modular V-8 replaced 5.0L in 1996.

Standard with both engines is the B&W T-5 five-speed manual transmission with the four-speed automatic AOD optional.

Other improvements for the 1994 model included dual airbags, standard driver's power seat, optional ABS brakes, standard tilt wheel, and an optional hardtop for the GT convertible.

Mustang Cobra

Just as the Mach 1 and Boss Mustangs replaced the GTs as the premier performance Mustang in the 1960s, the Cobra is doing the same thing in the 1990s.

Like the previous Cobra Mustangs, the 1994-95 versions feature a more powerful 5.0L V-8, rated at 240hp. The extra horsepower comes through the use of the so-called GT-40 cylinder heads, special intake manifold, a revised camshaft, 1.72:1 Crane rocker arms, and improved fuel injectors.

The suspension uses the base V-6 Mustang springs, along with a smaller front 0.98in anti-sway bar (1.18in/GT, 1.06in/base) and a larger rear one measuring 1.06in (.94in/GT, .83in/base). More significant are the PBR brakes, measuring 13.0in front/11.65in rear. These provide better braking than the stock 10.8in front/11.5in rear units. ABS is standard on the Cobra.

The Cobra uses a different front fascia, rear wing, and wheels; and the Cobra was available as a convertible for 1995, too. In the interior, the Cobra gets appropriate identification along with white gauges with black markings; the GT has white-on-black. All the standard power accessories and A/C are standard with the Cobra.

The Cobra R sits one inch lower than the stock Mustang Cobra. All were painted white. *Ford Motor Co.*

In order to fit in the Mustang engine compartment, special exhaust headers were required. These were installed by Roush Technologies. Here are some of the 351 V-8 engines awaiting shipment to the Dearborn Assembly plant. *Ford Motor Co.*

The result is a Mustang that accelerates faster but with a softer ride—which is actually preferable in everyday use. Color availability was limited to Crystal White, Black, or Rio Red.

Mustang Cobra R

The ultimate hot dog Mustang for 1995 was the Cobra R. Based on the Cobra (coupe body only), was built by Ford's SVT (Special Vehicle Team) to compete on various stock-type road race series. SVT built 107 Cobra R models in 1993; the problem was that most of these cars ended up in car collections instead of the track. To combat this tendency, Ford stipulated that anyone who bought a 1995 Cobra R had to be a member of a race sanctioning body, have a valid competition driver's license, and have a history of competition.

To keep up with and hopefully beat GM's Camaros and Firebirds, the R version got Ford's 5.8L (351ci) V-8 rated at 300hp and 365lbs/ft torque. Replacing the T-5 manual transmission was the stronger Tremec unit.

The suspension featured heavier front and rear springs, larger front and rear anti-sway bars, and Koni shocks and struts. The Cobra R used the same Cobra PBR brakes with larger 17x9in wheels mounting P255/45ZR17 B.F. Goodrich Comp T/A tires..

In keeping with its performance mission, the R did not have a rear seat, radio, A/C, power windows/locks/mirrors, sound insulation, or fog lights. It did come with a unique fiberglass hood. The only color available was white.

According to Ford, the R's top speed was estimated at 152mph with a 13.8sec quarter-mile time. Of the 250 Cobra Rs built, 232 were sold and eighteen were kept by Ford

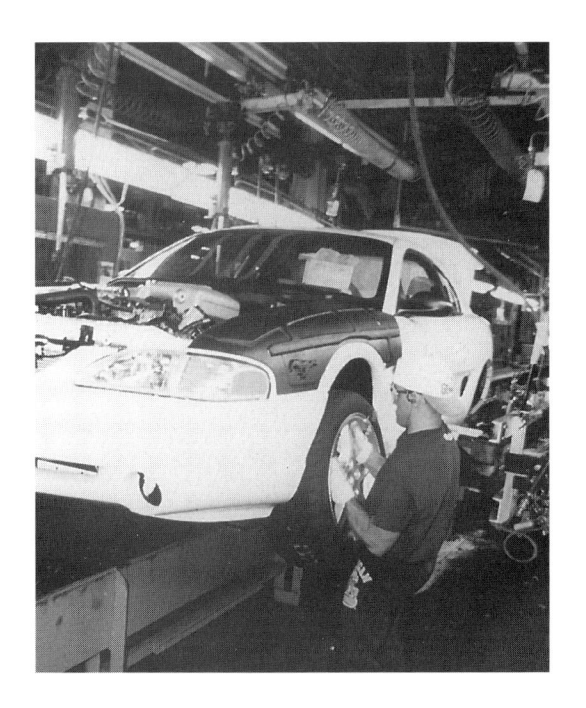

Another variation in the production process was the installation of the Mustang R wheels. These wheels and tires were too large to feed through the normal automated process so they had to be carried to the line for installation. *Ford Motor Co.*

for its press and engineering fleets. There is no doubt that the last eighteen cars, or at least most of them, will eventually end up in collector's hands.

Although Ford has built a Mustang that is quicker than the Camaro/Firebird, it has chosen not to make it available to the typical enthusiast. A Mustang that will beat a Z28 on the street is yet to come.

There are some interesting parallels between the Cobra R and the 1969-70 era Boss 429s. With the Boss 429, Ford shipped partially completed Mustangs to Kar Kraft for completion. With the Cobra R, Ford tried to do as much of the assembly in-house as

The final installation process was at MascoTech where the stock gas tank was replaced with a twenty gallon fuel cell. The standard cooling system components were also replaced. *Ford Motor Co.*

151

An interesting Mustang concept car that made the rounds in 1994 was the Mustang Mach III. Utilizing many Mustang styling cues, the Mach III roadster was powered by a 4.6L supercharged V-6. *Ford Motor Co.*

possible. The 351 engines were built at Ford's Windsor plant in Canada. They were then shipped to Roush Technologies for the installation of the exhaust system, because its assembly required considerable hand-work. The engines were then shipped to Ford's Dearborn Assembly plant where all Mustangs are built.

After the Cobra Rs were assembled at the plant, they were sent to MascoTech for the installation of the twenty gallon fuel cell and special cooling system.

This might sound as not being such a big deal, but in a typical plant where thousands and upon thousands of cars are built at a time, getting a small batch of essentially customized Mustangs built along with regular models is quite a logistical achievement.

Prospects

It will be quite some time before the fourth generation Mustangs are considered true collectibles. When they do, the Cobra convertible should be more desirable, followed by GT convertibles. It should be noted that one in three of 1994-95 Mustangs have been convertibles, so they may not command a very high premium over the coupe model, at least when compared to the first generation cars.

The 351 powered Cobra R is an exception; it is an instant collectible simply because of its rarity and uniqueness. Whoever has one isn't about to give it away, but then again, a good many of these Mustangs have seen race action (meaning they may be beat) and consequently, less expensive to obtain.

Chapter 13

1965–82 Shelby Mustangs

★★★★★	1965-66 Shelby GT350
★★★★	1967-70 Shelby GT350
★★★★✦	1967-70 Shelby GT500
★★★★★	1969-70 Shelby convertibles
★★★★	1980-82 Shelby convertibles

Six years ago, I wrote that there weren't any more inexpensive Shelby Mustangs for sale. This is now truer than ever. Of all Mustangs, it is the Shelby that has led the way in appreciation. They were and still are the premier Mustang image car. Perhaps the later 1967-70 Mustangs did not have the raw macho of the 1965-66 GT350s, but they

Compared to later Shelby Mustangs, the 1965 most closely resembled production Mustangs.

153

The stripes, hood scoop, relocated grille emblem, and 15 inch wheels really transformed the basic Mustang 2+2 body.

were considered better looking, easier to live with and faster when equipped with the big 428. The uniqueness and rarity of these cars were recognized from the start by Shelby owners and the result today is the Shelby American Automobile Club (SAAC). Through the club's efforts, recognition, preservation and appreciation of these classics have increased and translated directly into higher value. Although there are other clubs, SAAC offers the most for the Shelby enthusiasts.

The Shelby Mustangs were more than just restyled Mustangs. Looking back, with the Shelby as a great reminder, we can see how performance Mustangs have changed

This 1965 Shelby has the optional Cragar wheels.

over the years. Even though 1987-89 Mustang GTs now offer excellent performance, they just don't match the excitement, looks and presence generated by a Shelby. You just can't ignore a Shelby. That is why they are so popular today. Shelby Mustangs will continue to lead the way, and as a group, they are the best Mustang investment available.

1965 GT350

Through the years, the Shelby Mustangs have acquired an enviable reputation as being the fastest, most powerful and most performance-oriented of all Mustangs. This mystique is based on the 1965-66 Shelby Mustangs. These were truly an enthusiast's car as their sole purpose was to provide lots of performance. Finicky and temperamen-

The 1965 Shelby was a two seater. The spare, mounted on the rear shelf, took place of the production Mustang's rear seats.

Basic Mustang interior benefited from a wood steering wheel and special dash pod housing additional gauges. All 1965 Shelbys came with a black interior.

155

Standard wheels were silver-painted steel. However, the optional Cragars were very popular and added some visual punch to the 1965. Exhaust exited at the front of each rear wheel.

All Shelby Mustangs came with this data plate riveted to the left front fender. Be leery of a Shelby that doesn't have one.

A real powerhouse of an engine was the 306 hp 289 that ran the 1965 Shelby. The Export shock-tower brace and Monte Carlo bar added rigidity to the Mustang's structure, which improved handling. Note the lack of a power steering pump or power brake booster.

tal, they were definitely not for everybody and were as close to a streetable race car as was possible. They were fast, handled beautifully and looked the part.

The story has been told before, how Carroll Shelby, extremely successful with the Cobra roadster, got together with Ford. Ford, eager to improve its image as a performance, youth-oriented auto maker, needed a car to compete with GM's Corvette in road racing. The Shelby Mustang did both: improved Ford's image and won its class in SCCA's national road race championships from 1965 to 1967, as well as achieving numerous other race victories. Even today, original Shelby Mustangs are successfully raced.

Ford shipped partially completed 1965 Mustang fastbacks, only in Wimbledon White, to Shelby's plant in Los Angeles. These did not have rear seats, hoods or exhaust systems. The engine was the High Performance 289 ci 271 hp unit mated to an aluminum Borg Warner four-speed manual transmission with a 3.89:1 rear axle ratio. The cars were then re-engineered and modified to Shelby's specifications.

The appearance of the car was altered to distinguish it from regular production Mustangs. All Mustang identification and emblems were removed, save for the Mustang emblem on the front grille. The grille was changed, and the emblem was moved to the far left. A fiberglass hood with functional scoop took the place of the stock steel hood. A side stripe painted on the lower rocker panel had the GT350 nomenclature at the front. The familiar body stripes, beginning at the front valance panel and ending at the rear one, were optional and were sometimes installed by the selling Ford dealer.

The suspension was modified to greatly improve handling. In fact, the suspension of the street GT350 was identical to the full

Racing versions of the GT350 were designated GT350R. Some are still raced today. *Rick Kopec*

race version, the only difference being alignment specifications. A hefty, one-inch front stabilizer bar took the place of the stock part; special Pitman and idler arms for improved steering response were installed, as were the highly regarded Koni adjustable shock absorbers. Most importantly, the upper control arm suspension mounting points were lowered for better suspension geometry. In the engine compartment, a stronger brace from the firewall to shock tower (known as the Export Brace) and a Monte Carlo bar added the necessary rigidity to the Mustang's structure. In the rear, over-the-axle traction bars (to combat wheel hop during hard acceleration) and special rebound cables were attached to the axle housing. The brakes were modified as well. Manual front disc brakes and large 10×2½ inch rear drums with sintered metallic linings provided stopping power. The springs were also much stiffer.

The 271 hp 289 engine, already a good performer, got a thorough going-over. An aluminum high-rise intake manifold and 715 cfm Holley carburetor replaced the stock cast-iron manifold and Autolite carburetor. Steel Tri-Y design exhaust headers replaced the restrictive exhaust manifolds. The rest of the exhaust system consisted of straight-through mufflers with tailpipes exiting in front of the rear tires—very loud! A special cast-aluminum Cobra oil pan and Cobra valve covers improved engine appearance. The 289 was rated at 306 hp at 6000 rpm, but you could easily rev it to 7000 rpm.

Other modifications included a driveshaft safety loop and Detroit Locker differential. To further improve weight distribution, the battery was relocated to the trunk, but this modification was discontinued after the first 300 or so cars.

The standard Mustang black interior was modified with a special dash pod, which housed two additional gauges, an 8000 rpm tachometer and an oil pressure gauge. Three-inch competition seatbelts kept the driver in place, and an attractive genuine wood steering wheel replaced the stock plastic steering wheel. The 1965 Shelby Mustang did not

This 1965 R version GT350 has the rare aerodynamic rear window designed to improve top speed. *Alan Bolte*

Front apron was designed to duct more air through the radiator. This R has also been updated and modified. *Alan Bolte*

All R Shelby Mustangs came with a larger 34 gallon gas tank.

Not much changed on the 1966, 306 horsepower 289-ci engine. The engine, for all intents and purposes, was ready to race as it was delivered from the dealer.

Part of the reason why the Shelby Mustangs look so good is the tire-wheel combination. Tires that fill the wheelwells do more than anything else to enhance the performance image. *Rick Kopec*

A 1966 GT350 with Cragars. *Rick Kopec*

have a rear seat. In its place a fiberglass rear deck shelf was installed, which also housed the spare tire.

1965 Mustang GT350
Fastback body in Wimbledon White (color code M)
Fiberglass hood with scoop
Painted-on rocker panel stripes in Guardsman Blue (code F) with GT350 logo
Mustang gas cap
Mustang interior (black) with 3 inch competition seatbelts; rear seat deleted and replaced with fiberglass shelf and interior-mounted spare tire; genuine wood steering wheel
Dash pod housing tachometer and oil pressure gauge
15×6 inch silver-painted wheels with 7.75×15 Goodyear Blue Dot tires
306 hp 289 ci V-8 with chrome air cleaner, Cobra valve covers, intake manifold, oil pan, dual-point ignition, Holley 715 cfm carburetor and steel tube exhaust headers
4-speed aluminum case T-10 manual transmission
Side-exit dual exhaust system
Engine compartment Export brace and Monte Carlo bar
Lowered front suspension with 1 inch front sway bar
Front disc brakes
Quick-ratio steering
9 inch rear with 3.89:1 axle ratio
Detroit Locker no-spin differential
Over-the-axle traction bars
Koni shock absorbers
Desirable options
Guardsman Blue Le Mans body stripes
Cragar 15×6 mag wheels

Plain, silver-painted 15×6 inch steel wheels with chrome lug nuts were used with 7.75×15 Goodyear Blue Dot tires. Optional, and more attractive, were the Cragar 15×6 inch mags.

The full race version of the GT350 was known as the R model. The engine was modified further to increase horsepower to 350.

The 1966 Shelbys got the five-pod dash. Wood steering wheel was now an option.

1965 GT350 competition prepared version—R Model
The following are additions to street version:
Fiberglass front lower apron panel
Engine oil cooler
Large-capacity water radiator
Front and rear brake-cooling assemblies
34 gallon gas tank
3½ inch quick-fill cap
Electric fuel pump
Large-diameter exhaust pipes, no mufflers
5 magnesium 15×7 inch wheels
Revised wheelwells
Interior Safety Group (roll bar, shoulder harness, fire extinguisher, flame resistant interior, plastic rear window, aluminum-framed sliding plastic side windows)
Complete instrumentation (tachometer, speedometer, oil pressure and temperature, water temperature, fuel pressure)
Full Shelby American competition-prepared and dyno-tuned engine
Final track test and adjustments

The nose of the car differed with the installation of a front apron that improved radiator and brake airflow. The car was made lighter with the use of Plexiglass rear and side windows. Other race-only options included a larger 32 gallon gas tank, additional instrumentation, special racing seats, fireproof interior trim and a rear side scoop with brake cooling ducts. Wheels were 15×7 inch American Racing mags. All these, plus some other additions, cost $1,500 over the street GT350—a good deal indeed.

Visually the R model was similar to the street GT350. The result was strong product identification by the buyers—exactly what Ford wanted. Only thirty-seven R models were produced, making them one of the rarest Shelby Mustangs.

Performance for the street GT350 was exemplary. Weighing 2,800 pounds or so, it ran 0–60 mph times in about 6.5 seconds and quarter-mile times in the high-fourteen-second range. The car handled like a racer, but it was not an easy car to drive. The loud

Competition seatbelts were standard equipment on the 1966 Shelby. *Rick Kopec*

exhaust system, hard brake and clutch pedal pressure, extremely stiff suspension and lack of power steering limited its appeal to the diehard enthusiast. Accordingly, including the thirty-seven R models, only 562 Shelby Mustangs were sold in 1965.

1966 GT350

The year 1966 was a harbinger of the Shelby Mustang's fate. Ford felt that the Shelby Mustangs should try to pay their way, and in order to sell more, the Shelby Mustang began to move away from its original concept. By 1969, it was a styling testbed for Ford.

However, the 1966 Shelby was not all that different from the 1965. It was just toned down a bit. It was as fast as the 1965, and with the addition of the optional Paxton Supercharger, it had even better acceleration. Visually, only minor changes differentiated it. A side scoop was added to duct air to the rear brakes, and side quarter windows in place of the stock extractor vents enhanced the sleekness of the car. In addition, the 1966 Shelby could be had in colors other than white, such as red, blue, green and black.

The loud side exhaust system was replaced by a conventional system that exited behind the axle and used two conventional mufflers. The Detroit Locker differential and Koni

Another change for the 1966s was the Traction Master traction bars mounted beneath the rear leaf springs. The 1966 Shelbys were also available in colors other than white.

shocks were relegated to the options list. The springs were softened a bit.

The first 252 1966 GT350s were actually leftover 1965s updated to 1966 specifications. These still had the important A-arm suspension modification, while the rest of the 1966 Shelbys did not. As a cost-savings measure, the over-the-axle traction bars were replaced by those made by Traction Master Company, which fit underneath the springs.

The standard 1966 wheels were these grey-painted 14 inch Magnums.

Adding a little flair to this GT350 is the racing apron.

163

This is one of the rare, original 1966 Shelby convertibles. They all came with the optional Shelby wheels. *Jim Wicks*

In all other areas, however, it was still a true Shelby. The improved brakes and suspension and the powerful 306 hp 289 went unchanged. To further increase the GT350's appeal, the C-4 automatic three-speed transmission became optional.

The convertibles came with air conditioning, automatic transmissions and all other regular Shelby features. *Jim Wicks*

1966 Shelby Mustang GT350
Fastback body
Fiberglass hood with scoop (some all-steel hoods)
Rocker panel tape stripes with GT350 logo and Le Mans body stripes
GT 350 gas cap
Rear body quarter windows
Rear brake scoops
Mustang interior (black) with 3 inch competition seat belts; 5 gauge instrument cluster with dash-mounted tachometer; plastic woodgrain steering wheel
14×6 inch gray-painted Magnum 500 wheels with 6.95×14 Goodyear Blue Streak tires; 15 inch steel or Cragar wheels on early cars
306 hp 289 ci V-8 with Cobra oval air cleaner, valve covers, intake manifold and oil pan, dual-point ignition, steel tube exhaust headers
4-speed aluminum or iron case T-10 manual transmission
Conventional dual exhaust system
Engine compartment Export brace and Monte Carlo bar
1 inch front sway bar (early cars had lowered suspension)
Front disc brakes
Quick-ratio steering
9 inch rear with 3.89:1 axle ratio
Limited-slip differential
Desirable options
Paxton supercharger
Shelby alloy 14×6½ inch wheels
Woodgrain steering wheel
Koni shock absorbers
Fold-down rear seat

Although it looks like an original convertible, this is a replica.

A 1966 GT350H rental car.

Most GT350H were painted black with gold stripes.

The interior also became more hospitable. The 1966 Shelby Mustangs were equipped with rear seats (some had the fold-down seats), but another cost-cutting measure was the deletion of the wood steering wheel. It was replaced by a plastic woodgrain version, though the wood wheel was available optionally. The Shelby also got the five-pod

The 1966 GT350H.

The spare tire was relocated to the trunk on the 1966 GT350. Production rear seat took the place of the rear shelf.

Fold-down seat was optional on the 1966 GT350.

Mustang dash instrument cluster. The leftover 1965 cars came with the fifteen-inch Cragar mags or the painted steel wheels. The rest of the 1966s got 14×6 inch gray-painted Magnum 500 steel wheels with 6.95×14 Goodyear Blue Streak tires. Optional were the 14×6½ inch ten-spoke Shelby alloy wheels.

Six GT350 convertibles were made, but these were not originally available to the public. Each convertible was painted a different color: green, blue, white, red, pink and yellow. All convertibles were equipped with air conditioning, automatic transmission, wood steering wheel and the ten-spoke Shelby wheels. These are the rarest of all Shelby Mustangs.

Performance and handling of the 1966 Shelbys remained unchanged. What changes were made did not detract from the car. It was still a difficult car to drive, as close to a

GT350H wheels were chromed versions of the 14 inch Magnum 500s.

GT350Hs came with the same 306 hp 289 that other 1966 Shelby Mustangs had. You can be sure that these rental cars weren't babied.

race car as could be, with performance its sole purpose for being. Because it was a more civilized car, sales reached 2,380 units, including the six convertibles.

1966 GT350H

As a promotional ploy, Hertz Rent-A-Car ordered 1,000 Shelby Mustangs for use as rental cars and most of them were painted black with gold stripes. Slightly different from the regular production Shelby Mustangs, they used chrome Magnum 500 14×6 inch steel wheels and the automatic transmission cars had a 600 cfm Autolite carburetor rather than the 715 cfm Holley. Most Hertz cars were automatics. All Hertz cars received the GT350H designation.

Hertz claimed to have lost money on the venture, but more than made up for it with the youthful, performance image the Shel-

> **1966 Shelby Mustang GT350H**
> Gold rocker panel stripes with GT350H logo, gold body stripes 14×6 inch chrome Magnum 500 wheels

bys provided. In fact, Hertz again rented Shelby Mustangs in 1968-69, although these cars did not receive the GT350H designation.

The 1965-66 Shelby Mustangs are considered to be the purest in concept. Uncompromising, they delivered performance, with comfort and economy being secondary. Ford capitalized on this and with successive models was able to further tone down the car, increasing its appeal without hurting sales.

1967 GT350 and GT500

When the 1967 Mustang got its first major body restyle, so too did the Shelby Mustang. Based on the fastback body style,

The ultimate version of the 289, at least in production form, was equipped with the Paxton Supercharger. The supercharger was good for at least an additional 150 hp.

So, you wanted to impress your friends and neighbors? Then the 4×2 Weber carburetor setup was for you. Available as a dealer-installed option, this was the ultimate in carburetion.

The 1967 Shelby was a major restyle from regular production Mustangs. This GT500 Shelby has the rare original 427 engine.

Rear spoiler is pronounced on the 1967 Shelby. Side scoops add to the car's muscular, performance image.

the Shelby Mustang was extensively restyled to set it off further from the regular production Mustangs. The 1965-66 Shelby was easily identifiable as a Mustang; the 1967 was less so.

The nose of the car was extended via the liberal use of fiberglass components, to create a more pointed, meaner look. In many ways, the 1967 Shelby was the forerunner of later production Mustangs. A fiberglass hood, incorporating a large functional hood scoop, took the place of the stock steel hood. Two side scoops took the place of the stock air extractors, while the side brake scoops

The rear spoiler accentuated the rear. Taillights were 1967 Cougar. Stripes were dealer-installed.

Some 1967 Shelby Mustangs came with this headlight arrangement to comply with some states' lighting laws. In many ways, this setup is a precursor to the production 1969 Mustang nose.

The 1967 GT350 could be distinguished by the GT350 lettering on the rocker panel side stripes.

were carried over from 1966. The rear deck lid formed a ducktail spoiler and the revised taillight panel housed 1967 Cougar taillights. Headlight configuration differed from production Mustangs. Two outer low-beam headlights were used in conjunction with two high-beam units mounted within the grille opening. Most of these were mounted in the center, but to comply with certain states' headlight laws, some cars had the lights mounted at each end of the grille opening.

Stock were plain 15×6 inch steel wheels with hubcaps. You don't see many Shelbys with these hubcaps. Most 1967s have either the optional 15×7 inch Kelsey-Hayes Mag Star wheels or the 15×7 inch Shelby mags that were available later in the model year. Tires were E70×15 Goodyears.

The large hood-to-tail stripes were no longer part of the Shelby styling package.

Most factory 1967 photos showed the Shelby with hubcaps, which were standard. Optional were the Kelsey-Hays MagStar wheels.

The 1967 interior had two additional gauges mounted beneath dash in center. However, due to the dealer-installed air conditioning, they were relocated to the dash top on this GT500.

173

During the 1967 model year, these Shelby 15×7 inch mags became available.

The familiar rocker panel stripes with either the GT350 or GT500 designation were standard equipment. Exterior color selection expanded, and the interior could now be ordered in parchment or black. Two additional gauges—amps and oil pressure—were mounted under the dash, but more important, each Shelby Mustang got an integral roll bar and inertia-reel shoulder harness, the first in the American car industry. All Shelbys, beginning in 1967, had 140 mph speedometers and 8000 rpm tachometers.

The GT350 remained the same in the engine compartment. The 306 hp 289 was available with either a four-speed manual or a three-speed automatic. The Paxton supercharger remained a special-order option that provided almost big-block acceleration. A new Cobra air cleaner added distinction.

The big change was the addition of the 428 engine in the Shelby. These models got the GT500 designation. Externally similar to the 427 race engine, the 428 had a different bore and stroke (4.13×3.98) for excellent, torquey low-end response. The port and valve sizes were identical to the regular 390 cylinder heads. Pistons and crank were cast, but the rods were forged steel. Hydraulic lifters were used, but the main difference from other production 428s was the special induction system. A dual-plane aluminum intake manifold used two Holley 600 cfm

The standard engine on the GT350 was the 306hp 289. This particular 289 got a rare dual quad setup. The 1967 Shelbys came with this oval air cleaner.

The stock GT500 428 with two four-barrel carburetors was a very tight fit.

carburetors. These were mounted backwards and used a unique throttle linkage. All normal driving was done with the front carburetors' two primary barrels. The other six barrels would only be engaged under full throttle acceleration and this helped mileage quite a bit. The 428 was also fitted with Cobra valve covers and the Cobra air cleaner. It was rated at 355 hp at 5800 rpm.

The rare 427 was visually identical to the GT500's 428. Louvered hood came on some 1967 Shelby Mustangs.

Both the 427 and 428 used unique backward-mounted Holley carburetors. The Holleys on this 427 were not the original units.

Another rare setup was this Weber-equipped big-block.

Ford gave the 1968 Shelby an aggressively restyled nose. The 1967 and 1968 Shelby Mustangs epitomized what the late sixties muscle car phenomenon was all about, especially from the styling point of view.

1967 Shelby GT350, GT500
Fastback body
GT350, GT500 rocker panel tape stripe
Shelby grille, fender, deck lid and gas cap emblems
Fiberglass nose, hood with scoop, deck lid and end caps
Roof and side body scoops
Engines: GT350—306 hp 289 ci V-8 with Cobra air cleaner, valve covers, aluminum intake manifold and oil pan; GT500—355 hp 428 ci V-8 with Cobra air cleaner, Cobra Le Mans valve covers, aluminum intake manifold with 2×4V Holley carburetors
4-speed manual transmission
Power front disc brakes
Power steering
Competition Suspension
Dual exhaust system with chrome extensions
15×6 inch steel wheels and wheel covers with E70×15 tires
Deluxe interior and steering wheel
8000 rpm tachometer and 140 mph speedometer
Oil pressure gauge and ammeter
Integral roll bar with inertia shoulder harness

Desirable options
15×7 inch Mag Star styled steel wheels
15×7 inch Shelby alloy wheels
Air conditioning
Fold-down rear seat
Automatic transmission
Paxton supercharger (GT350 only)

The side scoops on the 1968s were unchanged.

It should also be noted that forty-seven GT500s came with the 427-ci Medium Riser engine (dealer installed). This was as close to a race engine as could be had from Ford. It featured forged steel crankshaft and rods, forged aluminum pistons, mechanical lifters and

The 1968 Shelby Mustangs came with louvered hoods.

177

The 1968 Shelby convertible makes an incredible visual impact. This is the potent GT500KR.

higher compression. The dual-quad intake manifold used two Holley 652 cfm carburetors. These were the rarest and fastest of all GT500s.

Suspension was strictly production Mustang, with heavier springs and shocks. The GT500 used a $^{15}/_{16}$ inch front stabilizer bar. Brakes were also production items, discs in

Grille opening on the 1968 was definitely no-nonsense. Resemblance to 1969 production Mustang is obvious.

T-Bird sequential taillights continued to be used on the 1968 Shelby. Note the rollbar.

The 1968 Shelby interior got this console with two additional gauges.

It seems that every domestic manufacturer used these wheel covers at one time or another. They were standard equipment on the 1968 Shelby.

the front and drums in the rear using regular linings. The availability of air conditioning as an option further transformed the Shelby.

The GT350 retained much of the flavor of the earlier GT350s. The lively, responsive 289 had to cope with about 350 pounds more weight, so acceleration times were slower. Handling was better than with regular production Mustangs, as the fiberglass hood helped front-to-rear weight distribution—fifty-three to forty-seven percent.

The GT500 handled pretty much like its cousin, the 390 GT Mustang. Both engines weighed the same in stock form, but the GT500's aluminum intake manifold and fiberglass hood took some of the weight off the front wheels. The GT500's forte was effortless acceleration with quarter-mile times in the low-fourteen-second range, depending on axle ratio and the driver of the car.

More popular on the 1968s are the optional Shelby alloy wheels.

The standard engine on the GT350 was the 250 hp 302. The aluminum high-rise intake manifold, Cobra valve covers and air cleaner looked good.

The GT500 428 came with only one Holley four-barrel carburetor but was rated 5 hp more than the 1967 GT500.

Ford's mid-year introduction was the GT500KR with the potent 428CJ engine. Note the flapper air cleaner and modified hood. Valve covers were aftermarket Shelby.

Although the Shelby bristled with visual performance cues such as scoops, spoilers, and big wheels and tires, it was no longer the Shelby Mustang that Carroll Shelby had envisioned. It was much more a compromise, and because of this sales hit 3,225 units for both models. The car was meant to retain the image and excitement of the original GT350 and at the same time appeal to a larger market segment. You could drive it everyday. It was by far the best Mustang available in 1967.

1968 GT350, GT500 and GT500KR

The Shelby line expanded in 1968, with the addition of an impressive convertible. Available with either a small-block or big-block, it accounted for about thirty percent of sales.

We all have a story of a car that we should have kept rather than sold. Mine concerns a 1968 GT350 convertible—but who would have thought, even in 1976, that these convertibles would become so desirable? Ouch!

In 1968, Ford took complete control of the Shelby operation and production of these cars was shifted to the A. O. Smith facility in Illinois. The nose of the Shelby was again restyled; in fact, Ford made much of this design, as the 1969 regular production Mustangs have more than a passing resemblance. Fiberglass hoods were once again used, with relocated scoops and air-extractor louvers to aid underhood heat dissipation. They also looked good. Headlight configuration reverted to a single seven-inch unit per side, with Lucas foglamps mounted inside the grille. The rear body and side scoops were carried over from 1967. The rear taillights,

The 1969 Shelby got an entirely new look. Front fenders and hood were fiberglass.

> **1968 Shelby Cobra GT350, GT500, GT500KR**
> Fastback or convertible
> GT350, GT500, GT500KR rocker panel tape stripes
> Cobra fender and gas cap emblems
> Fiberglass nose, hood with scoop, deck lid and end caps
> Roof and side body scoops
> Lucas foglamps mounted in front grille
> Chrome rocker panel molding
> Engines: GT350—250 hp 302 ci V-8 with Cobra air cleaner and valve covers, Holley carburetor; GT500—360 hp 428 ci V-8 with Cobra air cleaner, Cobra Le Mans valve covers, aluminum intake manifold with single Holley carburetor; GT500KR—335 hp 428CJ ci V-8 with Ram Air, Cobra Le Mans valve covers, cast-iron intake manifold with single Holley carburetor
> 4-speed manual transmission
> Power steering
> Power disc brakes
> 15×6 inch steel wheels and wheel covers with E70×15 tires
> Competition Suspension
> Staggered rear shock absorbers (GT500KR with 4-speed)
> Dual exhaust system with chrome quad extensions
> Deluxe interior and steering wheel
> 8000 rpm tachometer and 140 mph speedometer
> Console with oil pressure gauge and ammeter
> Integral roll bar with inertia shoulder harness
> Vinyl-covered roll bar (convertible only)
> **Desirable options**
> 15×7 inch Shelby alloy wheels
> Air conditioning
> Automatic transmission
> Fold-down rear seat (fastback only)
> Tilt steering wheel

this time 1965 Thunderbird units, were again sequential. Other embellishments included a chrome rocker panel cover beneath the side body stripe.

The interior used the production Mustang steering wheel. A console that housed two additional gauges was standard equipment. The roll bar, still standard, was encased in vinyl for the convertible.

The High Performance 289, dropped from regular production Mustangs, was deleted from the Shelby as well. In its place a production 302 became standard equipment on the GT350. It did use an aluminum intake manifold and a Holley 600 cfm carburetor to boost output to 250 hp. The distinctive Cobra valve covers and air cleaner were used on the 302.

The 428, for the GT500, was continued from 1967, but with some changes. The expensive dual-quad intake manifold and carburetors were replaced with a single Holley 650 cfm carburetor on an aluminum intake manifold. The 428 was now rated five horsepower more at 360 hp. During the model year, coinciding with the 428CJ's release, the GT500 was dropped and replaced by the GT500KR (King of the Road). The GT500KR had the more powerful 428CJ and came with all the necessary chassis modifications, but the engine was rated at only 355 hp.

A point worth considering with the 1968 GT500s is that some of the engines in these cars may be 390s because Ford ran out of 428s at one time during the year and substituted. As is well known, both engines are visually identical, but in terms of true horsepower, the 390 put out at least seventy-five horsepower less than the 428.

Suspension remained unchanged from regular production Mustangs. Handling, however, was better because the Shelby Mustang used 15×6 inch steel wheels with Goodyear E70×15 tires and the fiberglass hoods improved weight distribution. The aluminum 15×7 inch Shelby wheels were a popular option.

The GT500KR was clearly the fastest Shelby yet (except for the 1967 427), with quarter-mile times easily in the thirteen-second range.

Because Shelby Mustangs were even more distinctive than before, especially the convertible, they were perfectly suited for their targeted buyers. The car provided more than adequate handling, braking and impressive acceleration in a package that was more attractive and luxurious than regular Mustangs. Production increased to an all-time high of 4,450 units, with about sixty percent being big-block GT500s or GT500KRs.

1969-70 GT350 and GT500

These were the most extensively restyled Shelby Mustangs. No longer resembling production Mustangs, they featured a completely restyled nose section, which in many ways predated the 1971 Mustang. Totally under Ford control, the Shelby Mustangs were no longer the focus of Ford's performance activities, but visually, they conveyed

The 1969 Shelby grille no longer resembled the production Mustang's. Inertia reel harness was still standard equipment.

A 1969 Shelby convertible. All 1969s came with these Shelby mags.

The 1969 convertibles used the same roll bar as in 1968.

an overwhelming sense of power and performance.

The nose was lengthened by four inches. Fiberglass was still used for the hood, but the revised grille and bumper necessitated different front fenders, which were also made of fiberglass. Headlights were two seven-inch units with Lucas lamps mounted

Side scoop location on the fastbacks was larger, more pronounced than the production scoop.

On convertibles, the side scoop was lower.

The GT350 or GT500 designation was located on the front fenders.

beneath the front bumper. The hood incorporated five scoops and even the front fenders had a small scoop. Where the simulated side scoop was located on the production SportsRoofs, a larger side scoop took its place on the Shelby. The rear section again used 1965 Thunderbird sequential taillights, but the rear spoiler was even more pronounced. The exhaust system used a unique collector in the middle of the rear valence panel. The large reflective side stripes running the length of the car had either the GT350 or GT500 lettering on the front fender.

The Shelby got a redesigned wheel in 1969. Measuring 15×7 inches, it used an aluminum center with a steel rim. Standard tires were E70×15, but later in the year, the F60×15 Polyglas tires became available. Even at Concours shows, all you'll ever see are F60×15s.

The 1969 Shelby door panels were the Deluxe versions with appropriate identification.

The 1969 Shelby interior. Console top housed two additional gauges.

The standard GT350 engine was the 290 hp 351W. Cobra valve covers were owner-installed.

The interior was deluxe Mustang with the high-back bucket seats and appropriate Shelby identification. The standard console featured a different top that housed two additional gauges. As before, all Shelbys continued to come with a roll bar.

Mechanically, these Shelbys were identical to the 1969 Mach 1. The engine for the GT500 was the 428CJ-R rated at 335 hp. The GT350 got the four-barrel version of the new 351 Windsor engine, rated at 290 hp, but it used a more efficient aluminum intake manifold and had Ram Air as well. No Cobra valve covers or air cleaners on either engine were included. The 428CJ did get finned valve covers, however, while the 351 got plain finned aluminum valve covers and a chrome dipstick.

Although all the 1969 Shelby Mustangs were built in 1969—the last in November—not all were sold that year. About 600 were updated and sold as 1970 models by having their serial numbers changed. Two black stripes were added on the hood, and a Boss 302 type front spoiler was mounted. In all other respects, they were identical to the 1969s.

With increased emphasis on the Mach 1s and Bosses, Ford saw no reason to continue promoting the Shelby Mustang, especially

GT500s got the 428CJ-R engine.

1969-1970 Shelby GT350, GT500
Fastback or convertible
GT350 or GT500 reflective side stripes
Cobra grille, roof (fastback), rear quarter (convertible) emblems
Fiberglass hood, front fenders, deck lid and end caps
Side body scoops
Lucas foglamps mounted under front bumper
Color-keyed dual racing mirrors
Front spoiler (1970 only)
Black hood stripes (1970 only)
Engines: GT350—290 hp 351W V-8 with finned valve covers, alulminum intake manifold, Ram Air induction; GT500—335 hp 428CJ V-8 with finned valve covers, Holley carburetor, Ram Air induction
4-speed manual transmission
Power disc brakes
Power steering
15X7 styled wheels with Goodyear F60X15 Polyglas GT tires with RWL
Competition Suspension (staggered rear shock absorbers for 4-speed cars)
Dual exhaust system with unique exhaust collector
Deluxe interior with high-back bucket seats, center console, deluxe Rim-Blow steering wheel
8000 rpm tachometer and 140 mph speedometer
Oil pressure gauge and ammeter mounted on console top
Integral roll bar with inertia shoulder harness
Vinyl-covered roll bar (convertible only)
Desirable options
Fold-down rear seat (fastback only)
Air conditioning
Automatic transmission
Tilt steering wheel
Traction Lok differential

The 1970 Shelby Mustangs were 1969s that Ford "updated."

All 1969-70 Shelby Mustangs used this unique exhaust extractor. Taillights are the same as those found on 1968s.

The 1970s were updated by use of black hood stripes. *Dave Mathews*

as the 1969 model run could not be sold within the model year. The Shelby Mustang had made its mark years back, and since 1967, had served as a test-bed for Ford stylists.

It would have been interesting to see what Ford could have done with a 1971-73 Shelby Mustang.

1980-82 Shelby convertibles

From 1980 through 1982, Carroll Shelby produced an additional run of twelve convertibles, based on used 1966 Mustang convertibles. As his company was still a functioning entity, Shelby serial numbers could still be used. I suppose we can still consider these cars as Shelby Mustangs because they were built under Shelby's auspices, but they aren't quite the same thing as a Shelby built in 1966.

Removable Hardtop

Probably the most interesting and unique option on the 1995 Cobra convertible was

In addition to the hood stripes, all 1970s came with a Boss 302 type front spoiler.

A 1994 Pace Car convertible. All Pace Car models were painted Rio Red with a saddle interior and saddle top. Although this is a replica, the owner used the white logo that the track cars featured.

The ultimate Mustang—if a large engine is your bag. SVE built this 1994 concept that featured a 608-ci Boss 429 engine. The car is good for 10.6 seconds down the quarter-mile and runs close to 200 miles per hour.

The engine for the 1994 Boss is a comfortable fit in the car. The fuel injection system is custom made.

the removable hardtop. The top came with its own carrier for storing; and removing and replacing the top was a two-person operation. The factory hardtop cannot easily be retrofitted to other Mustang convertibles because the "A" pillar attachment point is different, and there are rear defroster wiring differences.

The top was supposed to be available to all models on the 1994 Mustang convertible, but none were produced. It was listed as a $1,545 option and was supposed to be a Cobra-only option, however, several 1995 GTs were sold with the removable hardtop. There were 500 tops installed on 1995 Cobras.

1994 Pace Car Replica

The 1994 Mustang was chosen to be the Official Pace Car of the 1994 Indianapolis 500. The most appropriate Mustang for this function was the high-performance Cobra Mustang GT. With the Pace Car decals on the side, these Mustangs shuffled the VIPs around the track.

Jack Roush built and prepped five Cobra Pace Cars. Three were used on the track, and the other two were used for display and parade functions.

The venerable 302-ci engine still powered the 1994–1995 Cobra. The 1995 model would be the last year this engine was available.

These Cobras did not have the standard five-speed manual transmission. They were fitted with Ford's four-speed AOD automatic transmission. In addition, the cars were equipped with a roll bar, a 15-gallon fuel cell, a Halon fire extinguisher system, and the usual emergency lights. The Cobra I.D. label was not used on the Pace cars.

There were 1,000 replicas built for sale to the public. All were painted Rio Red and had a saddle leather interior. The convertible top was also saddle. Besides the usual SVT certificate, each Pace Car received a sequentially numbered dash emblem.

The Pace Car decals were shipped in the trunk of each Cobra, and allowed each owner the option of applying them or not. One minor difference with the decals used on the original Pace Cars and the replicas was the Indianapolis Motor Speedway logo. On the track cars, the wheel on the logo is white, on the replicas the wheel is gray.

Prospects

The R cars and the convertibles are the most desirable Shelbys, followed by the 1965s and 1966s. Originality, authenticity and condition are of paramount importance, with an extremely small percentage of these cars modified from original to any great degree. It is important to remember that Shelby dealers offered a wide array of mechanical options, such as the Cobra kits. Any Shelby equipped with an exotic intake system such as Weber carburetors is especially valuable.

The only negative with such desirability and high appreciation is that there is a danger that these wonderful cars will become another commodity for investors to trade in. This is already happening with other makes where the single purpose for aquisition is a high return. Like all other Shelby Mustangs, the 1967s are in high demand. They do not fetch prices as high as do the 1965–66s, so are somewhat more affordable, but they'll never be cheaper than they are today. Noteworthy are the big-block powered GT500s as are the extremely rare 427 powered cars. Look for extensive documentation on any 427 powered GT500 as these were dealer installed. For the purist, the 1967 Shelby Mustangs are the last true Shelby Mustangs as Carroll Shelby still ran the show.

With so few Shelby convertibles made, they are the fastest appreciating of all 1968 Mustangs. I don't think there are many bargains left, but you never know. The 1968 fastbacks are similar in performance to the 1967 models, so it is basically a matter of taste. Some prefer the more aggressive look of the 1968s, while other enthusiasts prefer the 1967 because Carroll Shelby still had some control in their production.

The 1969s are just as much in demand as other Shelby Mustangs. Their unique styling and the fact that they are the last of the breed make them a good investment. As with the 1968s, the convertibles are highly sought after.

1965–70 Shelby Mustang

	1965–66	1967–68	1969–70
Wheelbase, in.	108	108	108
Track, front/rear, in.	57/57	58.1/58.1	58.5/58.5
Width, in.	68.2	70.9	71.8
Height, in.	51	49	50.3
Length, in.	181.6	186.6[1]	190.6
Curb weight, lb.	2,950	3,520[2]	3,670[3]
Weight distribution, % f/r	54.4/45.6	58/43	58/42

[1] *183.6 in 1968*
[2] *428 V-8*
[3] *428CJ V-8*

Chapter 14

1996–1998 Mustangs

★	Base Mustang
★★	GT Coupe
★★★	GT Convertible
★★★	Cobra Coupe
★★★★	Cobra Convertible

1996 Mustang

The SN-95 (the new identification of the Mustang) platform was carried over with minimal changes. There were two body styles, a coupe and a convertible, and significant changes under the hood for 1996.

The 5.0L V-8 was finally retired and replaced by a 4.6L version of Ford's modular V-8. The most unique feature of the modular V-8 was its chain-driven Single Overhead Camshaft Design (SOCD). The 4.6L features

A Mustang GT convertible. Except for the domed hood and rear taillights, there wasn't much change to the Mustang body.

The 1996 Cobra. The Mustang exhibits clean, crisp styling. It is small in size, yet large enough to remain attractive. Its arch-rival, the Camaro, is obviously larger but sales reached a low point and GM withdrew it from the market in 2002.

The Mystic paint color was available only on the 1996 Cobra. The paint has the ability to reflect four different colors, depending on the viewing angle.

The SOHC 4.6L that powered the Mustang GTs. Although it is rated at 260 horsepower, there is plenty of potential.

improved porting over the old 5.0L, and it has better breathing potential. The engine used a 65 mm throttle body with an 80 mm mass air sensor. It was rated at 215 horsepower at 5,000 rpm with 285 foot-pounds of torque at 4,800 rpm.

Besides the SOHC cylinder heads, the engine featured four-bolt main bearing caps for durability and a relatively square bore and stroke (3.55x3.54 inch) for good low-end torque. Different versions of the modular V-8 powered the GT and Cobra.

Ask anyone what they thought after they saw the engine compartment of a 19691970 Boss 429 Mustang for the first time. It was truly an amazing sight. A similar surprise can be encountered when someone takes a look at the engine of a 1996 Cobra Mustang. The Boss 429 engine is only an inch wider than the modular V-8.

There's little doubt that if it had been economically feasible, Ford would have continued using the 5.0L V-8. It was a cheap engine to manufacture, and best of all, it was tried and proven many times.

As stated earlier, both the Mustang GT and Cobra were equipped with the modular V-8 in 1996. However, the Cobra got the more powerful double-overhead cam 32-valve version, while the GT was equipped with the single-overhead cam version. This accounted for the 90 horsepower difference between the two engines. Another difference was that the GT version was made from cast

Another shot of the Cobra 4.6L. It is definitely the most modern V-8 to power Mustangs.

iron, while the Cobra's DOHC block and cylinder heads were cast in aluminum. The four-cam version was first introduced in 1993 in the Lincoln Mark VIII. The Cobra version of the engine had more than 100 modifications specifically designed to create more power.

Let's take a look at the cylinder block. Ford subcontracted the casting of the aluminum block to Teksid, a company located in Carmagnola, Italy. This company also casts for other European high-performance street and race cars. The casting was visually interesting because it incorporated a lot of cast-in ribbing for added strength. The pistons rode in cast-iron liners.

An interesting feature of the block, which added to its bottom-end strength, was the use of six bolts to retain the nodular iron main-bearing caps. The block's side skirts were similar to those found on Ford's old Y-block and FE-Series V-8s, in that they extend below the crankshaft's centerline. Four bolts went through the top of the cap into the cylinder block, and two more bolts through the side of the block into the cap similar to the way the old FE 427-ci engines or Chrysler's 426 Hemis were cross-bolted. This created a very rigid bottom-end structure.

Gerlach-Werke in Homburg/Saar, Germany, forged the crankshaft. The raw steel was heated to 2,300 degrees Fahrenheit and forged into shape under 8,000 tons of pressure. It was then shipped to Ford's Windsor engine plant in Ontario, Canada, where it

The Saleen Mustangs look great! Shown is a 1997 S281 model.

was machined and balanced. The crank's counterweights were placed opposite every throw, which contributed to the engine's smoothness.

The engine was equipped with a crank-wiping system. A unique windage tray wiped off the excess oil that tended to accumulate around the spinning crankshaft and directed it to the oil pan.

As one would expect, the Cobra engine was fitted with special connecting rods that featured a big end, heftier than other 4.6L variants. They were made of a powdered sinter-alloy that was compacted into the rough shape of a connecting rod, which was then "hot-struck" into the final shape. The 4.6L used specially coated pistons to reduce friction in the cylinders.

The cylinder heads made the Cobra engine unique. There are four kidney-shaped valves: two intake and two exhaust in each combustion chamber.

Above each secondary intake valve was a 34 mm butterfly port throttle. A cable was attached to each butterfly that was actuated by an electric motor. Below 3,250 rpm, the port throttle was closed and blocked any airflow to the secondary intake valve. Between 3,250 and 7,000 rpm, the EEC-V computer instructed the electric motor to open all the butterfly throttles to let more air into the combustion chamber while the fuel injectors inject more fuel. This allowed excellent airflow velocity at low engine speeds for sharp throttle response. At higher speeds, the engine utilized the superior flow capabilities of a four-valve cylinder head design. The twin, 57 mm bore throttle body also ensured that the engine had plenty of airflow. The mass-air sensor measures 80 mm.

A link-type timing chain connected the four hollow camshafts to the crankshaft. One chain per cylinder bank was connected to the crankshaft and the exhaust camshaft. Another chain connected the exhaust camshaft to the intake camshaft. All four chains used hydraulic tensioners to minimize chain slack. The camshafts did not rest directly on the valves. The cam lobes actuate roller finger followers that had a hydraulic valve-lash adjustment feature.

The 4.6L had a built-in engine oil cooler. The water-to-oil cooler is mounted on the left side of the block and it had the oil filter mounted on its end. Water returned from the radiator to the engine block and ran through the oil cooler to reduce oil temperature. Of course, if you used a good-quality synthetic oil, the oil temperature would be further reduced by 20 degrees.

The engine was finally assembled at Ford's Romeo, Michigan, engine plant by 12, two-person teams. Each engine had a plate affixed on the right valve cover with the initials of the two assemblers who put that particular engine together.

The engine output was 305 horsepower at 5,800 rpm with 300 foot-pounds of torque at 4,800 rpm. Generally speaking, the engine was more of a revving-type engine and lacked some of the low-end grunt often associated with the Windsor engines.

Along with the new engine, the 1996 V-8–powered Mustangs received a new transmission: the Borg-Warner T45 five-speed. The transmission, which weighed 110 pounds, had a torque rating of 320 foot-pounds. Unlike the T5, the bell housing was an integral part of the transmission casing which created a more rigid structure.

The GT's suspension was carried over for 1996. In the front, 400 to 505 pounds/inches variable rate springs were used with a 30 mm anti-sway bar. In the rear, 165 to 265 pounds/inches variable rate springs with a rear anti-sway bar measuring 25 mm were used. The rear bar for 1996 was 1 mm larger than the one used in 1995.

The brakes on all Mustangs were upgraded to a four-wheel disc setup. The front discs measured 10.8 inches, the rear discs were 10.5 inches. On the Cobra, the front vented discs measured 13 inches, while the rears were 11.65 inches in diameter. ABS was optional on the GT and standard on the Cobra.

Externally, all Mustangs received a new taillamp treatment that featured three vertical bars. Mustang GTs also were equipped with new GT 4.6L fender emblems.

There were some subtle changes to the Cobra's styling for 1996. The most noticeable change was the domed hood, which was necessary to clear the new 4.6L modular engine. The rear spoiler was also changed and Cobra lettering was stamped on the rear valance panel. A nice feature was the new 2.75-inch flared tailpipe outlets.

The available exterior paint colors were Crystal White, Black Clearcoat, Laser Red Tinted and the unusual Mystic paint. The Mystic paint exhibits four major metallic colors: green, amber, gold, and purple. The visual effect varies due to light intensity and the angle that it is viewed. The paint's color change capability is achieved via tiny transparent layered flakes in the paint's chemistry. These flakes act like prisms to break up white light into its component colors. The only traditional pigment used is black and Mystic is applied just like any other basecoat or clearcoat. This means that the paint has none of the color-match problems that are usually found in other special effects paints such as metalflakes, pearlescents, candy apples, and micas. Mystic was available only for the 1996 Cobra coupe.

1997–1998 Mustang

Except for a slight change in the front upper grille opening, there weren't many changes to the 1997 Mustang. The grille opening ducted more air to the new cross-the-board Mustang cooling system. All models had a wider and taller radiator and a larger diameter fan. A new parallel-flow air conditioning condenser was exclusive to the Cobra.

The Mustang GT received a new flecked interior fabric pattern, and medium graphite replaced the previous white interior that was used in 1996. New 17-inch wheels with a dark gray metallic center became optional on the GT.

For 1998, changes were again minimal to the Mustang line. The SOHC 4.6L received minor tweaks to produce 225 horsepower. The Cobra engine was still set to produce 305 horsepower.

Two new options were available in 1998. The GT Sport Group included the 17-inch, five-spoke aluminum wheels; hood and wraparound fender stripes; a leather-wrapped shift knob (manual transmission); and an engine oil cooler.

The V-6 Sport Appearance Group was available only on the base Mustang and included 16-inch cast aluminum wheels, rear spoiler, a leather-wrapped steering wheel, and a lower body-side accent stripe. This option gave the regular Mustang a stronger performance look.

The interior for the 1998 models was spruced up: A new leather pattern was used and the console was redesigned. The clock pod on the instrument panel was removed, and the clock was integrated into the radio display. A CD player also became part of the standard premium sound system.

The changes on the 1998 Cobra exterior were minimal. Visually, the most noticeable change was the wheels. They were the same as those used on the 1995 R model Cobras except the wheel cutouts were painted gray.

Saleen takes plenty of liberties with his cars. A super-charged 351-ci engine powers this 1998 model. There are plenty of scoops, vents, and spoilers, too.

Chapter 15

1999–2003 Mustangs

★	Base Mustang
★★	GT Coupe
★★★	GT Convertible
★★★	Bullitt GT Coupe
★★★	Cobra Coupe
★★★★	Cobra Convertible
★★★★★	2000 Cobra "R"

1999 Mustang

The Mustang was extensively restyled for this year, although the overall effect was evolutionary rather than revolutionary. Angular and definitive creases and lines replaced the smooth rounded lines of the 1994–1998 models. The side sculpturing was larger and led to a taller rear side scoop. All this was done to emulate the look of the first-generation Mustangs and still maintain a contemporary 1990s look. About the only

The 1999 Mustang. Its angular, definitive lines tend to grow on a person.

thing that didn't change from the 1994–1998 models was the roof. Overall, the Mustang became slightly longer and wider.

A subtle change was that the rear deck lid on all 1999 Mustangs was made from a sheet-molded compound (SMC) to reduce weight and eliminate the possibility of corrosion. The GT used a hood that incorporated a simulated hood scoop and also had larger, 3-inch exhaust tip extensions. The extensions previously measured 2.75 inches. All 1999 Mustangs also had a 35th anniversary version of the tri-color emblem on the sides of the front fenders.

There were considerable refinements and improvements to the 1999 Mustang chassis. A revised floor pan seal and additional foam in the rocker panels reduced road noise transmission, and subframe connectors on

The front end treatment on the 1999 Mustang GT. The band surrounding the front horse emblem and the hood treatment is visible. The hood scoop is just for show.

the convertible reducedæas Ford put itæ"mid-car shake." A 1.5-inch increase in the drive tunnel height at the rear axle resulted in more rear suspension travel.

New for the Mustang was an all-speed Traction Control System (TCS). The system was designed to control wheel spin under adverse road conditions. The system used the ABS sensors to detect when a drive wheel was spinning at a faster rate than the other wheel.

Although engine availability was unchanged from 1998, both Mustang engines received extensive modifications that resulted in more power. through the use of a new intake manifold and cylinder head improvements, the V-6 was upgraded to produce 190 horsepower at 4,000 rpm with 225 foot-pounds of torque at 3,000 rpm. A first-order balance shaft was added to improve engine smoothness.

The 4.6L modular V-8 was rated at 260 horsepower at 5,200 rpm with 302 foot-pounds of torque at 4,000 rpm. This was

The 4.6L modular V-8 engine. It's big no matter which way you look at it.

The independent suspension on the 1999 Cobra is quite a sight, plus it takes only four bolts to mount.

achieved through the use of higher lift and longer duration camshafts, coil-on-plug ignition, bigger valves, and a revised intake manifold that increased intake flow above 2,000 rpm.

Although the five-speed manual transmission was the same T45 that was used in previous years, for 1999 it was manufactured in red under license from Borg-Warner by Tremec. Both the V-6 and V-8 Mustangs were equipped with a 3.27:1 rear axle ratio for 1999.

A special 35th Anniversary Limited Edition package was made available for the GT. It included 17-inch wheels, black appliqué trim, a black tape treatment on the hood, and a special black and silver interior.

Besides the 1999 styling changes that were common to all Mustangs, the Cobra came with round fog lights in the lower front fascia and a regular hood, and the GT had a hood that incorporated a simulated hood scoop. Both the Cobra and GT had 3-inch exhaust tip extensions. All 1999 Mustang coupes received a SMC rear deck lid to save some weight.

Another difference with the GT and the Cobra was that the running horse emblem on the grille wasn't surrounded by a chrome band. Also, Cobras did not have the 35th anniversary tri-color bar emblem on the sides of the front fenders.

The 4.6L DOHC modular V-8 remained as the Cobra's sole powerplant. The engine, however, put out 15 horsepower and 17 foot-pounds of torque more than the 1998 version. This was due to different intake

The ultimate Mustang: the 2000 R model.

The 2000 R model is fitted with the 5.4L version of the modular engine. This means that it uses the SOHC heads and not the DOHC heads. Everything about the car means performance.

port geometry and a redesigned combustion chamber. These changes were said to make the fuel mixture tumble into the combustion chamber to promote better combustion. In addition, the engine benefited from stronger main and rod bearings.

The 1999 ignition system was changed to a coil-on-plug system to aid the combustion process. A better type of knock sensor—a differential linear type—replaced the former resonant knock sensor to better control any impending detonation.

The most significant change on the Cobra was the use of a new independent rear suspension system. The system used short and long arms that mounted on a tubular subframe. The lower arms were aluminum and the upper arms were steel. The subframe also held the aluminum differential case, which was borrowed from the Lincoln Mark VIII.

The independent rear mounted at the very same four mounting points that the regular Mustang solid-axle suspension did. Although the whole IRS setup weighed 80 pounds more than a comparable straight-axle rear, there was a 125-pound decrease in unsprung weight with the IRS. This resulted in a better ride and handling. The independent rear design allowed for much stiffer rear springs and the Cobra used 470 pounds/inches springs along with a 26 mm tubular anti-sway bar. The Mustang GT used 210 pounds/inches springs with a 23 mm solid bar.

Although the Cobra was supposed to be making 15 horsepower more, several enthusiast magazines reported that the 1999 Cobra seemed slower than previous models. Several Cobra owners had their cars dyno tested and the engine was found to be down on power. On August 6, 1999, Ford stopped

All three R models together—1993, 1995, and 2000.

the sale of any unsold Cobras sitting on the dealer's lots and recalled those sold to replace the intake manifold, the engine management computer, and the entire exhaust system from the catalytic converters. The result of all this was to eliminate the Cobra (except the R model) for the 2000 model year because a lot of time was spent getting the cars changed to reflect 320 horsepower.

2000 Mustang

Changes to the 2000 model Mustang were minimal. The color changes were the big deal of the year. These colors were Sunburst Gold, Laser Red, Performance Red, Amazon Green,

The infamous 4.6L DOHC. You can be sure that this 2001 version produces 320 horsepower.

The 2001 Mustang Cobra convertible.

Atlantic Blue, Bright Atlantic Blue, Electric Green, Black, Silver, and Crystal White.

The excitement that Mustang fanatics were following was the 2000 R model. Following the same pattern as the 1993 and 1995 R model versions, the 2000 R model was not equipped with any luxury options such as air conditioning, stereo, power windows, or power door locks. The standard seats were replaced with special Recaro versions that also incorporated a Cobra snake and R emblem on the head rest. The snake/R emblem was also used on the reverse indicator letter on the transmission shifter. Visually, the R model was distinguishable by the tall, rear wing spoiler and the front air dam. The low front air dam, which limited ground clearance, was easily removable for street use.

The engine used on the R model was a specially modified version of Ford's 5.4L SOHC V-8 mated to a six-speed manual transmission. It was rated at 385 horsepower. Its quarter-mile time was in the low 13s. All R models were painted red and production was limited to 300 units. There's no doubt that the R model created the excitement it was supposed to, and it was an instant collectible.

2001 Mustang

Besides the usual color changes (the colors offered were Zinc Yellow, Laser Red, Performance Red, Torch Red, True Blue, Tropic Green, Electric Green, Mineral Grey, Black, Satin Silver, and Oxford White) and the like, there was no major change on the Mustang line. Still, Ford did see fit to introduce a 2001 Mustang Bullitt GT inspired by the legendary 1968 Mustang Fastback that co-starred with Steve McQueen in the classic Warner Bros. film, *Bullitt*.

The 2001 Mustang Coupe.

A 2000 Mustang convertible and a GT Coupe. The Cobra was missing from the lineup, so Ford decided to fix the cars rather than sell more and subsequently deleted the model year. *Ford Motor Company.*

There were also engine and drivetrain changes. A new intake manifold used twin 57 mm throttle bodies and allowed for quicker throttle response and peak flow. Parasitic losses were reduced with the use of alternator and water pump pulleys. All Mustang Bullitts used a re-tuned exhaust system and a new TR3650 transmission that used a new 11-inch flywheel. These changes were all in the name of an increase in torque capacity and reduced clutch pedal efforts. All this resulted in a 5 horsepower increase to total 265 horsepower.

On the outside, subtle yet distinctive changes were made to the Mustang. These included the obvious hood scoop and 18 inch wheels that were patterned after the 1960s "Torque-Thrust"-type. It was a low-buck effort to produce something that was unique, and Ford succeeded.

2002 Mustang

The regular Mustang continued on, and the changes were minimal. Certainly such a lack of change is taken for granted today with body changes coming along every four or five years.

In 1968 Warner Bros. used a 1968 Mustang and a 1968 Hemi Charger in the "cops and robbers" film, *Bullitt*. The 1968 Mustang was expertly driven and filmed. With a few additions, the 2001 version of the Bullitt was introduced.
Ford Motor Company

All Cobra Mustangs received this rear spoiler as standard equipment, but it could be deleted at the owner's request. *Ford Motor Company*

The 2003 Cobra was released on February 7, 2002 as a 2003 model. Ford decided that rather than having a 2002 model, it would make the Cobra a 2003 model.

2003 Cobra Mustang

The 2003 Cobra was quite a bit different than the Mustangs that preceded it. Although it was still built on the same platform, the Cobra sported a new motoræa supercharged 4.6L 4V DOHC V-8. Power was increased to a level never before achieved in a production Mustang. With the addition of the supercharger, output was 390 horsepower at 6,000 rpm and 390 foot-pounds of torque at 3,500 rpm, and was 5 horsepower more than the 2000 Cobra R. And, for the first time, a six-speed manual transmission was standard on the Cobra as was a 3.55:1 rear-axle ratio.

Additional enhancements for 2003 included exterior design alterations to the front and rear fascia, hood (made from SMC), rocker moldings, and side scoops. Several changes were made to the interior appointments, including new multi-adjustable front seats trimmed in Nudo leather and Preferred suede.

Other changes were made for structural reasons: the cylinder block was cast iron rather than aluminum, the hood was redesigned with flow-through scoops to help vent hot air from the engine compartment, and the suspension and brakes were re-tuned for more power.

All this produced a considerably more powerful Mustang that was more desirable than previous models.

Prospects

The 1999–2002 period had been good for Mustang. The cars were developed, and now, they can be called "good" considering the age of the chassis— the platform is over 20 years old!

All these cars will appreciate, but it will take some time. The 2000 "R" model is a unique car that has all the marks of a collectible, even though later Cobra models had more power.

Appendices

Production figures

1965 Mustang (Early)
65A 2d Hardtop	92,705
76A Convertible	28,833
Total	121,538

1965 Mustang (Late)
63A 2d Fastback Standard	71,303
63B 2d Fastback Luxury	5,776
65A 2d Hardtop Standard	372,123
65B 2d Hardtop Luxury	22,232
65C 2d Hardtop Bench Seats	14,905
76A Convertible Standard	65,663
76B Convertible Luxury	5,338
76C Convertible Bench Seats	2,111
Total	559,451

1966 Mustang
63A 2d Fastback Standard	27,809
63B 2d Fastback Luxury	7,889
65A 2d Hardtop Standard	422,416
65B 2d Hardtop Luxury	55,938
65C 2d Hardtop Bench Seats	21,397
76A Convertible	56,409
76B Convertible Luxury	12,520
76C Convertible Bench Seats	3,190
Total	607,568

1967 Mustang
65A 2d Hardtop	325,853
65B 2d Hardtop Luxury	22,228
65C 2d Hardtop Bench Seats	8,190
63A 2d Fastback	53,651
63B 2d Fastback Luxury	17,391
76A Convertible	38,751
76B Convertible Luxury	4,848
76C Convertible Bench Seats	1,209
Total	472,121

1968 Mustang
63A 2d Fastback	33,585
63B 2d Fastback Deluxe	7,661
63C 2d Fastback Bench Seats	1,079
63D 2d Fastback Deluxe Bench Seats	256
65A 2d Hardtop	233,472
65B 2d Hardtop Deluxe	9,009
65C 2d Hardtop Bench Seats	6,113
65D 2d Hardtop Deluxe Bench Seats	853
76A Convertible	22,037
76B Convertible Deluxe	3,339
Total	317,404

1969 Mustang
63A 2d Fastback	56,022
63B 2d Fastback Deluxe	5,958
63C 2d Fastback Mach 1	72,458
65A 2d Hardtop	118,613
65B 2d Hardtop Deluxe	5,210
65C 2d Hardtop (Bench Seats)	4,131
65D 2d Hardtop Deluxe (Bench Seats)	504
65E 2d Hardtop Grande	22,182
76A Convertible	11,307
76B Convertible Deluxe	3,439
Total	299,824

1970 Mustang
63A 2d Fastback	39,470
65A 2d Hardtop	77,161
76A Convertible	6,199
63B 2d Fastback	6,464
65B 2d Hardtop	5,408
76B Convertible	1,474
63C Fastback Mach 1	40,970
65E 2d Hardtop Grande	13,581
Total	190,727

1971 Mustang
Standard
65D 2d Hardtop	65,696
63D 2d Fastback	23,956
76D Convertible	6,121

Grande
65F 2d Hardtop	17,406

Mach 1
63R 2d Fastback	36,499
	Total 149,678

1972 Mustang
Standard
65D 2d Hardtop	57,350
63D 2d Fastback	15,622
76D Convertible	6,401

Grande
65F 2d Hardtop	18,045

Mach 1
63R 2d Fastback	27,675
	Total 125,093

1973 Mustang
Standard
63D 2d Fastback Hardtop	10,820
65D 2d Hardtop	51,480
76D 2d Convertible	11,853

Grande
65F 2d Hardtop	25,274

Mach 1
63R 2d Fastback Hardtop	35,440
	Total 134,867

1974 Mustang
Standard
60F 2d Hardtop	177,671
69F 3d Hardtop	74,799

Ghia
60H 2d Hardtop	89,477

Mach 1
69R 2d Hardtop	44,046
	Total 385,993

1975 Mustang
60F 2d Hatchback	85,155
69F 3d Hatchback	30,038

Ghia
60H 2d Hatchback	52,320

Mach 1
69R 3d Hatchback	21,062
	Total 188,575

1976 Mustang
60F 2d Notchback	78,508
69F 3d Hatchback	62,312
60H 2d Notchback Ghia	37,515
69R 3d Hatchback Mach 1	9,232
	Total 187,567

1977 Mustang
60F 2d Notchback	67,783
69F 3d Hatchback	49,161
60H 2d Notchback Ghia	29,510
69R 3d Hatchback Mach 1	6,719
	Total 153,173

1978 Mustang
60F 2d Notchback	81,304
69F 3d Hatchback	68,408
60H 2d Notchback Ghia	34,730
69R 3d Hatchback Mach 1	7,968
	Total 192,410

1979 Mustang
66B 2d Sedan	156,666
61R 3d Fastback	120,535
66H 2d Sedan Ghia	56,351
61H 3d Fastback Ghia	36,384
	Total 369,936

1980 Mustang
66B 2d Sedan	128,893
66H 2d Sedan Ghia	23,647
61H 3d Fastback Ghia	20,285
61R 3d Fastback Sport	98,497
	Total 271,322

1981 Mustang
66B 2d Sedan	77,458
66H 2d Sedan Ghia	13,422
61H 3d Fastback Ghia	14,273
61R 3d Fastback Sport	77,399
	Total 182,552

1982 Mustang
66B 2d Sedan	45,316
66H 2d Sedan Ghia	5,828
61H 3d Fastback Ghia	9,926
61B 3d Fastback Sport	69,348
	Total 130,418

1983 Mustang
66B 2d Sedan	33,201
2d Convertible	23,438
61B 3d Fastback	64,234
	Total 120,873

1984 Mustang
66B 2d Sedan	37,680
2d Convertible	17,600
61B 3d Fastback	86,200
	Total 141,480

1985 Mustang
66B 2d Sedan	56,781
2d Convertible	15,110
61B 3d Fastback	84,623
	Total 156,514

1986 Mustang
66B	2dr Sedan	83,774
	2dr Convertible	22,946
61B	3dr Fastback	1167,690
	Total	224,410

1987 Mustang
66B	2dr Sedan	43,257
	2dr Convertible	21,447
61B	3dr Fastback	94,441
	Total	159,145

1988 Mustang
66B	2dr Sedan	53,221
	2dr Convertible	32,074
61B	3dr Fastback	125,930
	Total	211,225

Source: Ford Motor Company

1989 Mustang
66B	2dr Sedan	50,560
	2dr Convertible	43,244
61B	3dr Hatchback	116,965
	Total	210,769

1990 Mustang
66B	2dr Sedan	22,503
	2dr Convertible	26,958
61B	2dr Hatchback	78,728
	Total	128,189

1991 Mustang
66B	2dr Sedan	19,447
	2dr Convertible	21,513
61B	2dr Hatchback	57,777
	Total	98,737

1992 Mustang
66B	2dr Sedan	15,717
	2dr Convertible	23,470
61B	2dr Hatchback	40,093
	Total	79,280

1993 Mustang
66B	2dr Sedan	24,851
	2dr Convertible	27,300
61B	2dr Hatchback	62,077
	Total	114,228

1994 Mustang
2dr Coupe	48,873
2dr Convertible	19,471
2dr Coupe GT	35,137
2dr Convertible GT	27,582
2dr Coupe Cobra	5,009
2dr Convertible Cobra	1,002
Total	137,074

1995 Mustang
2dr Coupe	86,379
2dr Convertible	18,593
2dr Coupe GT	47,088
2dr Convertible GT	16,668
2dr Coupe GTS	6,370*
2dr Coupe Cobra	4,255
2dr Convertible Cobra	1,003
Total	180,356

* Included in GT Coupe

1996 Mustang
2dr Coupe	61,187
2dr Convertible	15,246
2dr GT Coupe	31,624
2dr GT Convertible	17,917
2dr Cobra Coupe	7,496
2dr Cobra Convertible	2,510
Total	135,980

1997 Mustang
2dr Coupe	56,812
2dr Convertible	11,606
2dr GT Coupe	18,464
2dr GT Convertible	11,413
2dr Cobra Coupe	6,961
2dr Cobra Convertible	3,088
Total	108,344

1998 Mustang
2dr Coupe	99,801
2dr Convertible	21,254
2dr GT Coupe	28,789
2dr GT Convertible	17,024
2dr Cobra Coupe	5,174
2dr Cobra Convertible	3,480
Total	175,522

1999 Mustang
2dr Coupe	73,180
2dr Convertible	19,299
2dr GT Coupe	19,634
2dr GT Convertible	13,699
2dr Cobra Coupe	4,040
2dr Cobra Convertible	4,055
Total	133,907

2000 Mustang
2dr Coupe	121,026
2dr Convertible	41,368
2dr GT Coupe	32,328
2dr GT Convertible	20,224
2dr Cobra Coupe	354
2dr Cobra Convertible	100
Total	215,400

2001 Mustang

2dr Coupe	75,321
2dr Convertible	30,399
2dr GT Coupe	32,511*
2dr GT Convertible	18,336
2dr Cobra Coupe	3,867
2dr Cobra Convertible	3,384
Total	163,818

Includes 5,582 Bullitt Mustangs

GT

1965	15,079
1966	25,517
1967	24,079
1968	17,458
1969	4,973
Total	87,106

Mach 1

1969	72,458
1970	40,970
1971	36,499
1972	27,675
1973	35,440
Total	213,042

K Engine 1965-1967

1965	7,273
1966	5,469
1967	489
Total	13,231

390 Engine

1967	29,457
1968	10,650
1969	10,549
Total	50,656

Boss

1969	Boss 302		1,628
	Boss 429		859*
	Total		2,487
1970	Boss 302		7,013
	Boss 429		499
	Total		7,512
1971	Boss 351		1,806
	Grand Total		11,805

Includes 2 Boss Cougars

428 CJ/SCJ Engine

1968-1/2	2,870
1969	15,133
1970	3,959
Total	21,962

429 CJ/SCJ Engine

1971	1,865

351-HO Engine

1972	398

Shelby

1965 Shelby GT350

GT350 Street Prototype	1
GT350 Street Cars	520
1966 Prototype	1
Drag Cars	4
Competition Prototype	2
Competition Production Cars	34
Total	562

1966 Shelby GT350

GT350	1,368
GT350H	999
GT350H Prototype	1
Paxton Prototype	1
Drag Cars	4
GT350 Convertibles	4
Notchback Prototype	1
Notchback Race Cars	20
Total	2,398

1967 Shelby

GT500 Notchback Prototype	1
GT350 Fastbacks	803
GT350 Fastbacks Hertz Cars	224
GT350 Convertibles	404
GT500 Fastbacks	1,044
GT500 Convertibles	402
GT500KR Fastbacks	1,053
GT500KR Convertibles	517
GT500KR Convertibles Hertz Cars	1
Shelby Notchback Race Cars	5
Total	4,454

1969–1970 Shelby

1969 Shelby	2,361
1970 Shelby	789
Barrier test Cars & prototypes	3
GT350 Fastbacks	935
GT350 Fastback Hertz Cars	152
GT350 Convertibles	194
GT500 Fastbacks	1,534
GT500 Convertibles	335
1969 Boss 302 Fastback Racers	5
Total	6,308

Mustang engines 1965–2003

Year	Type	Cubic inches	Bore x stroke	Hp@rpm	Torque (lbs.-ft) & rpm	CR	Carb	Engine code
1964½	I-6	170	3.50 x2.94	101@4400	156@2400	8.7	1V	U
	V-8	260	3.80 x2.87	164@4400	258@2200	8.8	2V	F
	V-8	289	4.00 x2.87	210@4400	300@2800	9.0	4V	A
1965	I-6	200	3.68 x3.13	120@4400	190@2400	9.2	1V	T
	V-8	289	4.00 x2.87	200@4400	282@2400	9.3	2V	C
	V-8	289	4.00 x2.87	225@4800	305@3200	10.0	4V	A
	V-8	289	4.00 x2.87	271@6000	312@3400	10.5	4V	K
	V-8	289 (Shelby)	4.00 x2.87	306@6000	329@4200	10.5	4V	K
1966	I-6	200	3.68 x3.13	120@4400	190@2400	9.2	1V	T
	V-8	289	4.00 x2.87	200@4400	282@2400	9.3	2V	C
	V-8	289	4.00 x2.87	225@4800	305@3200	10.0	4V	A
	V-8	289	4.00 x2.87	271@6000	312@3400	10.5	4V	K
	V-8	289 (Shelby)	4.00 x2.87	306@6000	329@4200	10.5	4V	K
1967	I-6	200	3.68 x3.13	120@4400	190@2400	9.2	1V	T
	V-8	289	4.00 x2.87	200@4400	282@2400	9.3	2V	C
	V-8	289	4.00 x2.87	225@4800	305@3200	10.0	4V	A
	V-8	289	4.00 x2.87	271@6000	312@3400	10.5	4V	K
	V-8	289 (Shelby)	4.00 x2.87	306@6000	329@4200	10.5	4V	K
	V-8	390	4.05 x3.78	320@4800	427@3200	10.5	4V	S
	V-8	427 (Shelby)	4.23 x3.78	425@6000	480@3700	11.0	8V	Q or S
	V-8	428 (Shelby)	4.13 x3.98	355@5400	420@3200	10.5	8V	Q or S
1968	I-6	200	3.68 x3.13	115@4400	190@2400	8.8	1V	T
	V-8	289	4.00 x2.87	195@4600	288@2600	8.7	2V	C
	V-8	302	4.00 x3.00	230@4800	310@2800	10.0	4V	J
	V-8	302 (Shelby)	4.00 x3.00	250@4800	310@2800	10.0	4V	J
	V-8	390	4.05 x3.78	325@4800	427@3200	10.5	4V	S
	V-8	427	4.23 x3.78	390@4600	460@3200	10.9	4V	W
	V-8	428CJ	4.13 x3.98	335@5600	440@3400	10.6	4V	R
	V-8	428 (Shelby)	4.13 x3.98	360@5400	420@3200	10.5	4V	S
1969	I-6	200	3.68 x3.13	115@2800	190@2200	8.8	1V	T
	I-6	250	3.68 x3.91	155@4000	240@1600	9.0	1V	L
	V-8	302	4.00 x3.00	220@4600	300@2600	9.5	2V	F
	V-8	302 Boss	4.00 x3.00	290@5800	290@4300	10.5	4V	G
	V-8	351W	4.00 x3.50	250@4600	355@2600	9.5	2V	H
	V-8	351W	4.00 x3.50	290@4800	385@3200	10.7	4V	M
	V-8	390	4.05 x3.78	320@4600	427@3200	10.5	4V	S
1969	V-8	428CJ, CJ-R	4.13 x3.98	335@5600	440@3400	10.6	4V	Q-CJ, R-CJ-R
	V-8	429 Boss	4.36 x3.59	375@5200	450@3400	10.5	4V	Z
1970	I-6	200	3.68 x3.13	120@4400	190@2900	8.0	1V	T
	I-6	250	3.68 x3.91	155@4000	240@1600	9.0	1V	L
	V-8	302	4.00 x3.00	220@4600	300@2600	9.5	2V	F
	V-8	302 Boss	4.00 x3.00	390@5800	290@4300	10.5	4V	G
	V-8	351W	4.00 x3.50	250@4600	355@2600	9.5	2V	H
	V-8	351C	4.00 x3.50	250@4600	355@2600	9.5	2V	H
	V-8	351C	4.00 x3.50	300@5400	380@3400	11.0	4V	M
	V-8	428CJ, CR-R	4.13 x3.98	335@5600	440@3400	10.6	4V	Q-CJ, R-CJ-R
	V-8	429 Boss	4.36 x3.59	375@5200	450@3400	10.5	4V	Z

Year	Type	Cubic inches	Bore x stroke	Hp@rpm	Torque (lbs.-ft) & rpm	CR	Carb	Engine code
1971	I-6	250	3.68 x3.91	145@4000	232@1600	9.0	1V	L
	V-8	302	4.00 x3.00	210@4600	296@2600	9.0	2V	F
	V-8	351C	4.00 x3.50	240@4600	350@2600	9.0	2V	H
	V-8	351C-CJ	4.00 x3.50	280@5400	370@3400	9.0	4V	M
	V-8	351C	4.00 x3.50	285@5400	370@3400	10.7	4V	M
	V-8	351C Boss	4.00 x3.50	330@5400	370@4000	11.7	4V	R
	V-8	429CJ-R	4.36 x3.59	370@5400	450@3400	11.3	4V	C
	V-8	429SCJ-R	4.36 x3.59	375@5600	450@3400	11.3	4V	J, C, non ram air
1972	I-6	250	3.68 x3.91	98@3400	197@1600	8.0	1V	L
	V-8	302	4.00 x3.00	140@4000	239@2000	8.5	2V	F
	V-8	351C	4.00 x3.50	177@4000	284@2000	8.6	2V	H
	V-8	351C-CJ	4.00 x3.50	266@5400	301@3600	9.0	4V	Q
	V-8	351C-HO	4.00 x3.50	275@6000	286@3800	9.2	4V	R
1973	I-6	250	3.68 x3.91	99@3600	184@1600	8.0	1V	L
	V-8	302	4.00 x3.00	141@4000	242@2000	8.0	2V	F
	V-8	351C	4.00 x3.50	177@4000	284@2000	8.6	2V	H
	V-8	351C-CJ	4.00 x3.50	266@5400	301@3600	9.0	4V	Q
1974	I-4	140	3.781x3.126	88@5000	116@2600	8.4	2V	Y
	V-6	170.8	3.66 x2.70	105@4600	140@3200	8.2	2V	Z
1975	I-4	140	3.781x3.126	88@5000	116@2600	9.0	2V	Y
	V-6	170.8	3.66 x2.70	105@4600	140@3200	8.7	2V	Z
	V-8	302	4.00 x3.00	140@4200	234@2200	8.0	2V	F
1976	I-4	140	3.781x3.126	88@5000	116@2600	9.0	2V	Y
	V-6	170.8	3.66 x2.70	105@4600	140@3200	8.7	2V	Z
	V-8	302	4.00 x3.00	140@4200	234@2200	8.0	2V	F
1977	I-4	140	3.781x3.126	92@5000	121@3000	9.0	2V	Y
	V-6	170.8	3.66 x2.70	103@4300	149@2800	8.7	2V	Z
	V-8	302	4.00 x3.00	134@3600	247@1800	8.4	2V	F
1978	I-4	140	3.781x3.126	88@4800	118@2800	9.0	2V	Y
	V-6	170.8	3.66 x2.70	90@4200	143@2200	8.7	2V	Z
	V-8	302	4.00 x3.00	139@3600	250@1600	8.4	2V	F
1979	I-4	140	3.781x3.126	88@4800	118@2800	9.0	2V	Y
	I-4	140 Turbo	3.781x3.126	132@5500	142@3500	9.0	2V	W
	V-6	170.8	3.66 x2.70	109@4800	142@2800	8.7	2V	Z
	I-6	200	3.68 x3.13	85@3600	154@1600	8.5	1V	T
	V-8	302	4.00 x3.00	140@3600	250@1800	8.5	2V	F
1980	I-4 MT	140	3.781x3.126	88@4800	118@2800	9.0	2V	A
	I-4 AT	140	3.781x3.126	90@4800	125@2600	9.0	2V	A
	I-4 Turbo	140	3.781x3.126	135@6000	143@2800	9.0	2V	T
	I-6	200 MT	3.68 x3.13	91@3800	160@1600	8.6	1V	B
	I-6	200 AT	3.68 x3.13	94@4000	157@2000	8.6	1V	B
	V-8	255	3.68 x3.00	119@3800	194@2200	8.8	2V	D
1981	I-4	140	3.781x3.126	88@4600	118@2600	9.0	2V	A
	I-6	200	3.68 x3.13	94@4000	158@1400	8.6	1V	B
	V-8	255	3.68 x3.00	120@3400	205@2200	8.2	2V	D
1982	I-4	140	3.781x3.126	88@4600	118@2600	9.0	2V	A
	I-6	200	3.68 x3.13	94@4000	158@1400	8.6	1V	B
	V-8	255	3.68 x3.00	120@3400	205@2200	8.2	2V	D
	V-8	302	4.00 x3.00	157@4200	240@2400	8.4	2V	F
1983	I-4	140	3.781x3.126	88@4600	118@2600	9.0	1V	A
	V-6	232	3.814x3.388	112@4000	175@2600	8.6	2V	3
	V-8	302 HO	4.00 x3.00	175@4000	245@2400	8.3	4V	F

Year	Type	Cubic inches	Bore & stroke	Hp@rpm	Torque (lbs.-ft) & rpm	CR	Carb	Engine Code
1984	I-4	140	3.781x3.126	88@4000	122@2400	9.0	1V	A
	I-4 Turbo GT	140	3.781x3.126	145@4600	180@3600	8.0	EFI	T
	I-4 SVO	140	3.781x3.126	175@4400	210@3000	8.0	EFI	T
	V-6	232	3.814x3.388	120@3600	205@1600	8.6	EFI	3
	V-8	302 HO	4.00 x3.00	175@4000	245@2200	8.3	4V	F
	V-8	302 HO	4.00 x3.00	205@4400	265@3200	8.3	4V-dual exhaust	F
	V-8	302 HO	4.00 x3.00	165@3800	245@2000	8.3	EFI	F
1985	I-4	140	3.781x3.126	88@4400	122@2600	9.5	1V	A
	I-4 SVO	140	3.781x3.126	205@5000	248@3000	8.0	EFI	T
	V-6	232	3.814x3.388	120@3600	205@1600	8.7	EFI	3
	V-8	302 HO	4.00 x3.00	165@3800	245@2000	8.4	EFI	F
	V-8	302 HO	4.00 x3.00	210@4600	265@3400	8.4	4V-dual exhaust	F
1986	I-4	140	3.78 x3.126	88@4400	122@2600	8.3	1V	A
	I-6	232	3.81 x3.39	120@3600	205@1600	8.7	EFI	3
	V-8	302 HO	4.00 x3.00	200@4600	265@3400	8.4	EFI	F
1987	Same as 1986 with the following exceptions:							
	V-8	302 HO	4.00 x3.00	220@4400	300@3000	8.4	EFI	F
	V-8	302 HO	4.00 x3.00	225@4400	300@3000	8.4	EFI	M
1988	Same as 1987							
1992	V-8	302 HO	4.00 x3.00	225@4200	300@3200	9.0:1	EFI	E
1993	V-8	302 Cobra	4.00 x3.00	235@4600	280@4000	9.0:1	EFI	D
	V-8	302 HO	4.00 x3.00	205@4200	275@3000	9.0:1	EFI	E
1995	V-6	3.8L	3.81 x3.39	145@4000	215@2500	9.0:1	EFI	
	V-8	302 HO	3.81 x3.39	215@4200	285@3400	9.0:1	EFI	E
	V-8	302 Cobra	3.81 x3.39	240@4600	285@4000	9.0:1	EFI	O
	V-8	5.8L R	4.00 x3.50	300@4800	365@4800	9.0:1	EFI	
1994	V-6	3.8l	3.81x3.39	145@4000	215@2500	9.0:1	EFI	4
	V-8	5.0l	4.00x3.00	215@4200	284@3400	9.0:1	EFI	E
	V-8	5.0l	4.00x3.00	240@4600	285@4000	9.0:1	EFI	D
1995	V-6	3.8l	3.81x3.39	145@4000	215@2500	9.0:1	EFI	4
	V-8	5.0l	4.00x3.00	215@4200	285@3400	9.0:1	EFI	E
	V-8	5.0l	4.00x3.00	240@4600	285@4000	9.0:1	EFI	D
	V-8	5.8l	4.00x3.50	300@4800	365@4800	9.0:1	EFI	C
1996	V-6	3.8l	3.81x3.39	150@4000	215@2500	9.0:1	EFI	4
	V-8	4.6l	3.55x3.54	215@5000	285@4800	9.0:1	EFI	W
	V-8	4.6l	3.55x3.54	305@5800	300@4800	9.85	EFI	V
1997	V-6	3.8l	3.81x3.39	150@4000	215@2500	9.0:1	EFI	4
	V-8	4.6l	3.55x3.54	215@2500	285@4800	9.0:1	EFI	W
	V-8	4.6l	3.55x3.54	305@5800	300@4800	9.85	EFI	V
1998	V-6	3.8l	3.81x3.39	150@4000	215@2500	9.0:1	EFI	4
	V-8	4.6l	3.55x3.54	225@5000	285@4800	9.0:1	EFI	W
	V-8	4.6l	3.55x3.54	305@5800	300@4800	9.85	EFI	V
1999	V-6	3.8l	3.81x3.39	190@4000	225@3000	9.0:1	EFI	4
	V-8	4.6l	3.55x3.54	260@5000	302@4000	9.0:1	EFI	W
	V-8	4.6l	3.55x3.54	320@6000	317@4750	9.85	EFI	V
2000	V-6	3.8l	3.81x3.39	190@4000	225@3000	9.0:1	EFI	4
	V-8	4.6l	3.55x3.54	260@5000	302@4000	9.0:1	EFI	W
	V-8	5.4l	3.55x4.17	385@5700	385@4500	9.6:1	EFI	H
2001	V-6	3.8l	3.81x3.39	190@4000	225@3000	9.0:1	EFI	4
	V-8	4.6l	3.55x3.54	260@5000	302@4000	9.0:1	EFI	W
	V-8	4.6l	3.55x3.54	265@5000	302@4000	9.0:1	EFI	W
	V-8	4.6l	3.55x3.54	320@6000	317@4750	9.85	EFI	V
2002	V-6	3.8l	3.81x3.39	190@4000	225@3000	9.0:1	EFI	4
	V-8	4.6l	3.55x3.54	260@5000	302@4000	9.0:1	EFI	W
2003	V-8	4.6l	3.55x3.54	390@6000	390@3500	8.5:1	EFI	W

High performance Mustang engines

225 HP 289 4V

- VIN letter code .... A
- BHP @ rpm .... 225 @ 4800
- Torque @ rpm .... 305 @ 3200
- Bore, in. 4.00
- Stroke, in. 2.87
- Cubic displacement 289
- Compression ratio .... 10.0 to 1
- Fuel required .... Premium
- Carburetor .... Autolite 4V
- CFM rating 470
- Intake port, in. 1.04x1.94
- Exhaust port, in. .... .96x1.24
- Intake/exhaust valve diameter, in. 1.78/1.45
- Camshaft type .... Hydraulic
- Valve lift, intake/exhaust, in. .... .360/.380
- Duration, intake/exhaust, degrees 266/244
- Normal oil pressure @ rpm .... 35-55 psi @ 2000
- Used on .... 1965-67 Mustang GT

271 HP 289 HIGH PERFORMANCE

- VIN letter code .... K
- BHP @ rpm .... 271 @ 6000
- Torque @ rpm .... 312 @ 3400
- Bore, in. 4.00
- Stroke, in. 2.87
- Cubic displacement 289
- Compression ratio .... 10.5 to 1
- Fuel required .... Premium
- Carburetor .... Autolite 4V
- CFM rating 480
- Intake port, in. 1.04x1.94
- Exhaust port, in. .... .96x1.24
- Intake/exhaust valve diameter, in. 1.78/1.45
- Camshaft type .... Mechanical
- Valve lift, intake/exhaust, in. .... .460/.460
- Duration, intake/exhaust, degrees 310/310
- Normal oil pressure @ rpm .... 35-55 psi @ 2000
- Used on .... 1965-67 Mustang GT

200 HP 289 2V

- VIN letter code C
- BHP @ rpm .... 200 @ 4400
- Torque @ rpm .... 282 @ 2400
- Bore, in. 4.00
- Stroke, in. 2.87
- Cubic displacement 289
- Compression ratio .... 9.3 to 1
- Fuel required .... Regular
- Carburetor .... Autolite 2V
- CFM rating 350
- Intake port, in. 1.04x1.94
- Exhaust port, in. .... .96x1.24
- Intake/exhaust valve diameter, in. 1.78/1.45
- Camshaft type .... Hydraulic
- Valve lift, intake/exhaust, in. .... .360/.380
- Duration, intake/exhaust, degrees 266/244
- Normal oil pressure @ rpm .... 35-55 psi @ 2000
- Used on .... 1967 Mustang GT

320 HP 390GT 4V

- VIN letter code .... S
- BHP @ rpm .... 320 @ 4600
- Torque @ rpm .... 427 @ 3200
- Bore, in. 4.05
- Stroke, in. 3.78
- Cubic displacement 390
- Compression ratio .... 10.5 to 1
- Fuel required .... Premium
- Carburetor .... Holley 4V (1967),
  Autolite 470 cfm (1969)
- CFM rating 600
- Intake port, in. 1.34x1.93
- Exhaust port, in. 1.28x1.84
- Intake/exhaust valve diameter, in. 2.04/1.57
- Camshaft type .... Hydraulic
- Valve lift, intake/exhaust, in. .... .481/.490
- Duration, intake/exhaust, degrees 270/290
- Normal oil pressure @ rpm .... 35-65 psi @ 2000
- Used on .... 1967 Mustang GT, 1969 Mustang GT, 1969 Mach 1

230 HP 302 4V

- VIN letter code .... J
- BHP @ rpm .... 230 @ 4800
- Torque @ rpm .... 310 @ 3800
- Bore, in. 4.00
- Stroke, in. 3.00
- Cubic displacement 302
- Compression ratio .... 10.0 to 1
- Fuel required .... Premium
- Carburetor .... Autolite 4V
- CFM rating 470
- Intake port, in. 1.04x1.94
- Exhaust port, in. .... .96x1.24
- Intake/exhaust valve diameter, in. 1.78/1.45
- Camshaft type .... Hydraulic
- Valve lift, intake/exhaust, in. .... .360/.380
- Duration, intake/exhaust, degrees 266/244
- Normal oil pressure @ rpm .... 35-55 psi @ 2000
- Used on .... 1968 Mustang GT

335 HP 428CJ RAM AIR 4V

VIN letter code	R, Q for non-Ram Air
BHP @ rpm	335 @ 5200
Torque @ rpm	440 @ 3400
Bore, in.	4.13
Stroke, in.	3.98
Cubic displacement	428
Compression ratio	10.6 to 1
Fuel required	Premium
Carburetor	Holley 4V
CFM rating	735
Intake port, in.	1.34x2.34
Exhaust port, in.	1.28x1.84
Intake/exhaust valve diameter, in.	2.09/1.65
Camshaft type	Hydraulic
Valve lift, intake/exhaust, in.	.481/.490
Duration, intake/exhaust, degrees	270/290
Normal oil pressure @ rpm	35-60 psi @ 2000
Used on	1968 Mustang GT, 1968 Shelby Cobra GT500KR, 1969-70 Shelby Mustang GT500, 1969-70 Mach 1

325 HP 390 GT 4V

VIN letter code	S
BHP @ rpm	325 @ 4800
Torque @ rpm	427 @ 3200
Bore, in.	4.05
Stroke, in.	3.78
Cubic displacement	390
Compression ratio	10.5 to 1
Fuel required	Premium
Carburetor	Holley 4V
CFM rating	600
Intake port, in.	1.34x1.93
Exhaust port, in.	1.28x1.84
Intake/exhaust valve diameter, in.	2.04/1.57
Camshaft type	Hydraulic
Valve lift, intake/exhaust, in.	.481/.490
Duration, intake/exhaust, degrees	270/290
Normal oil pressure @ rpm	35-65 psi @ 2000
Used on	1968 Mustang GT

390 HP 427 4V

VIN letter code	W
BHP @ rpm	390 @ 5600
Torque @ rpm	460 @ 3200
Bore, in.	4.23
Stroke, in.	3.78
Cubic displacement	427
Compression ratio	10.9 to 1
Fuel required	Premium
Carburetor	Holley 4V
CFM rating	650
Intake port, in.	1.34x1.93
Exhaust port, in.	1.28x1.84
Intake/exhaust valve diameter, in.	2.04/1.57
Camshaft type	Hydraulic
Valve lift, intake/exhaust, in.	.481/.490
Duration, intake/exhaust, degrees	270/290
Normal oil pressure @ rpm	35-60 psi @ 2000
Used on	1968 Mustang GT

250 HP 351W 2V

VIN letter code	H
BHP @ rpm	250 @ 4600
Torque @ rpm	355 @ 2600
Bore, in.	4.00
Stroke, in.	3.50
Cubic displacement	351
Compression ratio	9.5 to 1
Fuel required	Regular
Carburetor	Autolite 2V
CFM rating	350
Intake port, in.	1.76x1.94
Exhaust port, in.	.96x1.24
Intake/exhaust valve diameter, in.	1.84/1.54
Camshaft type	Hydraulic
Valve lift, intake/exhaust, in.	.425/.450
Duration, intake/exhaust, degrees	256/270
Normal oil pressure @ rpm	35-60 psi @ 2000
Used on	1969-70 Mach 1

290 HP 351W 4V

VIN letter code	M
BHP @ rpm	290 @ 4800
Torque @ rpm	385 @ 3200
Bore, in.	4.00
Stroke, in.	3.50
Cubic displacement	351
Compression ratio	10.7 to 1
Fuel required	Premium
Carburetor	Autolite 4V
CFM rating	470
Intake port, in.	1.76x1.94
Exhaust port, in.	.96x1.24
Intake/exhaust valve diameter, in.	1.84/1.54
Camshaft type	Hydraulic
Valve lift, intake/exhaust, in.	.425/.450
Duration, intake/exhaust, degrees	256/270
Normal oil pressure @ rpm	35-60 psi @ 2000
Used on	1969 Mach 1, 1969-70 Shelby GT350

250 HP 351C 2V

VIN letter code	H
BHP @ rpm	250 @ 4600
Torque @ rpm	355 @ 2600
Bore, in.	4.00
Stroke, in.	3.50
Cubic displacement	351
Compression ratio	9.5 to 1
Fuel required	Regular
Carburetor	Autolite 2V
CFM rating	350
Intake port, in.	1.40x2.02
Exhaust port, in.	1.38x1.84
Intake/exhaust valve diameter, in.	2.05/1.66
Camshaft type	Hydraulic
Valve lift, intake/exhaust, in.	.400/.400
Duration, intake/exhaust, degrees	258/266
Normal oil pressure @ rpm	35-60 psi @ 2000
Used on	1970 Mach 1

300 HP 351C 4V

VIN letter code	M
BHP @ rpm	300 @ 5400
Torque @ rpm	380 @ 3400
Bore, in.	4.00
Stroke, in.	3.50
Cubic displacement	351
Compression ratio	11.0 to 1
Fuel required	Premium
Carburetor	Autolite 4V
CFM rating	470
Intake port, in.	1.75x2.50
Exhaust port, in.	1.74x2.00
Intake/exhaust valve diameter, in.	2.19/1.71
Camshaft type	Hydraulic
Valve lift, intake/exhaust, in.	.420/.450
Duration, intake/exhaust, degrees	268/280
Normal oil pressure @ rpm	35-60 psi @ 2000
Used on	1970 Mach 1

210 HP 302 2V

VIN letter code	F
BHP @ rpm	210 @ 4600
Torque @ rpm	296 @ 2600
Bore, in.	4.00
Stroke, in.	3.00
Cubic displacement	302
Compression ratio	9.0 to 1
Fuel required	Regular
Carburetor	Motorcraft 2V
CFM rating	350
Intake port, in.	1.04x1.94
Exhaust port, in.	.96x1.24
Intake/exhaust valve diameter, in.	1.78/1.45
Camshaft type	Hydraulic
Valve lift, intake/exhaust, in.	.360/.380
Duration, intake/exhaust, degrees	266/244
Normal oil pressure @ rpm	35-55 psi @ 2000
Used on	1971 Mach 1

285 HP 351C 4V

VIN letter code	M
BHP @ rpm	285 @ 5400
Torque @ rpm	370 @ 3400
Bore, in.	4.00
Stroke, in.	3.50
Cubic displacement	351
Compression ratio	10.7 to 1
Fuel required	Premium
Carburetor	Motorcraft 4V
CFM rating	470
Intake port, in.	1.75x2.50
Exhaust port, in.	1.74x2.00
Intake/exhaust valve diameter, in.	2.19/1.71
Camshaft type	Hydraulic
Valve lift, intake/exhaust, in.	.420/.450
Duration, intake/exhaust, degrees	268/280
Normal oil pressure @ rpm	35-60 psi @ 2000
Used on	1971 Mach 1

370 HP 429CJ-R 4V

VIN letter code	J
BHP @ rpm	370 @ 5400
Torque @ rpm	450 @ 3400
Bore, in.	4.36
Stroke, in.	3.59
Cubic displacement	429
Compression ratio	11.3 to 1
Fuel required	Premium
Carburetor	Rochester Quadrajet
CFM rating	700
Intake port, in.	2.12x2.86
Exhaust port, in.	1.32x2.24
Intake/exhaust valve diameter, in.	2.25/1.72
Camshaft type	Hydraulic
Valve lift, intake/exhaust, in.	.506/.506
Duration, intake/exhaust, degrees	282/296
Normal oil pressure @ rpm	35-75 psi @ 2000
Used on	1971 Mach 1

375 HP 429SCJ-R 4V

VIN letter code	J
BHP @ rpm	375 @ 5600
Torque @ rpm	450 @ 3400
Bore, in.	4.36
Stroke, in.	3.59
Cubic displacement	429
Compression ratio	11.3 to 1
Fuel required	Premium
Carburetor	Holley 4V
CFM rating	780
Intake port, in.	2.12x2.86
Exhaust port, in.	1.32x2.24
Intake/exhaust valve diameter, in.	2.25/1.72
Camshaft type	Mechanical
Valve lift, intake/exhaust, in.	.509/.509
Duration, intake/exhaust, degrees	300/300
Normal oil pressure @ rpm	35-75 psi @ 2000
Used on	1971 Mach 1

275 HP 351HO 4V

VIN letter code	R
BHP @ rpm	275 @ 6000
Torque @ rpm	286 @ 3800
Bore, in.	4.00
Stroke, in.	3.50
Cubic displacement	351
Compression ratio	9.2 to 1
Fuel required	Regular
Carburetor	Motorcraft 4V
CFM rating	750
Intake port, in.	1.75x2.50
Exhaust port, in.	1.74x2.00
Intake/exhaust valve diameter, in.	2.19/1.71
Camshaft type	Mechanical
Valve lift, intake/exhaust, in.	.490/.490
Duration, intake/exhaust, degrees	275/275
Normal oil pressure @ rpm	35-60 psi @ 2000
Used on	1972 Mach 1

140 HP 302 2V

VIN letter code	F
BHP @ rpm	140 @ 4000
Torque @ rpm	239 @ 2000
Bore, in.	4.00
Stroke, in.	3.00
Cubic displacement	302
Compression ratio	8.5 to 1
Fuel required	Regular
Carburetor	Motorcraft 2V
CFM rating	350
Intake port, in.	1.04x1.94
Exhaust port, in.	.96x1.24
Intake/exhaust valve diameter, in.	1.78/1.45
Camshaft type	Hydraulic
Valve lift, intake/exhaust, in.	.360/.380
Duration, intake/exhaust, degrees	266/244
Normal oil pressure @ rpm	35-55 psi @ 2000
Used on	1972-73 Mach 1

177 HP 351C 2V

VIN letter code	H
BHP @ rpm	177 @ 4000
Torque @ rpm	284 @ 2000
Bore, in.	4.00
Stroke, in.	3.50
Cubic displacement	351
Compression ratio	8.6 to 1
Fuel required	Regular
Carburetor	Motorcraft 2V
CFM rating	350
Intake port, in.	1.40x2.02
Exhaust port, in.	1.38x1.84
Intake/exhaust valve diameter, in.	2.05/1.66
Camshaft type	Hydraulic
Valve lift, intake/exhaust, in.	.400/.400
Duration, intake/exhaust, degrees	258/266
Normal oil pressure @ rpm	35-60 psi @ 2000
Used on	1972-73 Mach 1

266 HP 351CJ 4V

VIN letter code	Q
BHP @ rpm	266 @ 5400
Torque @ rpm	301 @ 3600
Bore, in.	4.00
Stroke, in.	3.50
Cubic displacement	351
Compression ratio	9.0 to 1
Fuel required	Regular
Carburetor	Motorcraft 4V
CFM rating	470
Intake port, in.	1.75x2.50
Exhaust port, in.	1.74x2.00
Intake/exhaust valve diameter, in.	2.19/1.71
Camshaft type	Hydraulic
Valve lift, intake/exhaust, in.	.481/.490
Duration, intake/exhaust, degrees	270/290
Normal oil pressure @ rpm	35-60 psi @ 2000
Used on	1972-73 Mach 1

290 HP BOSS 302 4V

VIN letter code	G
BHP @ rpm	290 @ 5800
Torque @ rpm	290 @ 4300
Bore, in.	4.00
Stroke, in.	3.00
Cubic displacement	302
Compression ratio	10.5 to 1
Fuel required	Premium
Carburetor	Holley 4V
CFM rating	780
Intake port, in.	1.75x2.50
Exhaust port, in.	1.74x2.00
Intake/exhaust valve diameter, in.	1.71/2.23 (1969), 1.71/2.19 (1970)
Camshaft type	Mechanical
Valve lift, intake/exhaust, in.	.477/.477
Duration, intake/exhaust, degrees	290/290
Normal oil pressure @ rpm	35-60 psi @ 2000
Used on	1969-70 Boss 302 Mustang

375 HP BOSS 429 4V

VIN letter code	Z
BHP @ rpm	375 @ 5200
Torque @ rpm	450 @ 3400
Bore, in.	4.36
Stroke, in.	3.59
Cubic displacement	429
Compression ratio	10.5 to 1
Fuel required	Premium
Carburetor	Holley 4V
CFM rating	735
Intake port, in.	2.36x2.36
Exhaust port, in.	1.68x2.04
Intake/exhaust valve diameter, in.	2.28/1.90
Camshaft type	Hydraulic (1969), Mechanical (1970)
Valve lift, intake/exhaust, in.	.506/.506 (1969), .509/.509 (1970)
Duration, intake/exhaust, degrees	282/296 (1969), 300/300 (1970)
Normal oil pressure @ rpm	45-60 psi @ 2000
Used on	1969-70 Boss 429

330 HP BOSS 351 4V

VIN letter code	R
BHP @ rpm	330 @ 5400
Torque @ rpm	370 @ 4000
Bore, in.	4.00
Stroke, in.	3.50
Cubic displacement	351
Compression ratio	11.7 to 1
Fuel required	Premium
Carburetor	Motorcraft 4V
CFM rating	750
Intake port, in.	1.75x2.50
Exhaust port, in.	1.74x2.00
Intake/exhaust valve diameter, in.	2.19/1.71
Camshaft type	Mechanical
Valve lift, intake/exhaust, in.	.477/.477
Duration, intake/exhaust, degrees	290/290
Normal oil pressure @ rpm	35-60 psi @ 2000
Used on	1971 Boss 351

425 HP MEDIUM RISER 427 8V

VIN letter code	Not listed on VIN
BHP @ rpm	425 @ 6000
Torque @ rpm	480 @ 3700
Bore, in.	4.23
Stroke, in.	3.78
Cubic displacement	427
Compression ratio	11.6 to 1
Fuel required	Premium
Carburetor	Holley 2x4V
CFM rating	1304
Intake port, in.	1.34x2.34
Exhaust port, in.	1.28x1.84
Intake/exhaust valve diameter, in.	2.19/1.73
Camshaft type	Mechanical
Valve lift, intake/exhaust, in.	.500/.500
Duration, intake/exhaust, degrees	306/306
Normal oil pressure @ rpm	35-65 psi @ 2000
Used on	1967 Shelby GT500

306 HP 289 HP SHELBY

VIN letter code	K
BHP @ rpm	306 @ 6000
Torque @ rpm	329 @ 4200
Bore, in.	4.00
Stroke, in.	2.87
Cubic displacement	289
Compression ratio	10.5 to 1
Fuel required	Premium
Carburetor	Holley 4V
CFM rating	715
Intake port, in.	1.04x1.94
Exhaust port, in.	.96x1.24
Intake/exhaust valve diameter, in.	1.78/1.45
Camshaft type	Mechanical
Valve lift, intake/exhaust, in.	.460/.460
Duration, intake/exhaust, degrees	310/310
Normal oil pressure @ rpm	35-55 psi @ 2000
Used on	1965-67 Shelby GT350 Mustang

250 HP 302 4V

VIN letter code	J
BHP @ rpm	250 @ 4800
Torque @ rpm	310 @ 2800
Bore, in.	4.00
Stroke, in.	3.00
Cubic displacement	302
Compression ratio	10.0 to 1
Fuel required	Premium
Carburetor	Holley 4V
CFM rating	600
Intake port, in.	1.04x1.94
Exhaust port, in.	.96x1.24
Intake/exhaust valve diameter, in.	1.78/1.45
Camshaft type	Hydraulic
Valve lift, intake/exhaust, in.	.360/.380
Duration, intake/exhaust, degrees	266/244
Normal oil pressure @ rpm	35-55 psi @ 2000
Used on	1968 Shelby Cobra GT350

355 HP 428 8V SHELBY

VIN letter code	Q or S
BHP @ rpm	355 @ 5400
Torque @ rpm	420 @ 3200
Bore, in.	4.13
Stroke, in.	3.98
Cubic displacement	428
Compression ratio	10.5 to 1
Fuel required	Premium
Carburetor	Holley 2x4V
CFM rating	1200
Intake port, in.	1.34x2.34
Exhaust port, in.	1.28x1.84
Intake/exhaust valve diameter, in.	2.04/1.57
Camshaft type	Hydraulic
Valve lift, intake/exhaust, in.	.481/.490
Duration, intake/exhaust, degrees	270/290
Normal oil pressure @ rpm	35-65 psi @ 2000
Used on	1967 Shelby GT500

360 HP 428 4V SHELBY

VIN letter code	S
BHP @ rpm	360 @ 5400
Torque @ rpm	420 @ 3200
Bore, in.	4.13
Stroke, in.	3.98
Cubic displacement	428
Compression ratio	10.5 to 1
Fuel required	Premium
Carburetor	Holley 4V
CFM rating	650
Intake port, in.	1.34x2.34
Exhaust port, in.	1.28x1.84
Intake/exhaust valve diameter, in.	2.04/1.57
Camshaft type	Hydraulic
Valve lift, intake/exhaust, in.	.481/.490
Duration, intake/exhaust, degrees	270/290
Normal oil pressure @ rpm	35-65 psi @ 2000
Used on	1968 Shelby Cobra GT500

Specifications

Mustang specifications

	1964–66	1967–68	1969–70	1971–73	1974–78	1979–1993	1994–2003
Wheelbase, in.	108	108	108	109	96.2	100.4	101.3
Track, frt./rear, in.	56/56	58.1/58.1	58.5/58.5	61.5/61.5	55.6/55.8	56.6/57	60.6/59.1
Width, in.	68.2	70.9	71.8	74.1	70.2	69.1	71.8
Height, in.	51	51.8	50.3	50.1	50.3	51.9	52.9
Length, in.	181.6	183.6	187.4	189.5[1]	175	179.0	181.5
Curb weight, lb.	2,860 (289)	2,980 (302)	3,625 (428CJ)	3,560 (351CJ)	3,290 (302)	2,861 (140)[2]	3,065 (3,276 GT)
Wt. dist., % f/r	53/47 (289)	56/44 (302)	59/41 (428CJ)	56.5/43.5 (351)	59/41	57/43[3]	57/43

[1] – 193.8 in 1973
[2] – 3,075 with 302
[3] – 59/41 with 302

Clubs

Mustang Club of America
3588 Highway 138
PMB 365
Stockbridge, GA 30281
www.mustang.org
   The largest Mustang club open to all Mustangs. Publishes the magazine *The Mustang Times* monthly, Over 100 regional groups.

Mustang Owners Club International
2720 Tennessee N.E.
Albuquerque, NM 87110
   Open to all Mustangs. Publishes *The Pony Express* a monthly newsletter.

Shelby American Automobile Club
P.O. Box 788
Sharon, CT 06069
www.saac.com
   The largest Shelby Mustang club in the country. Publishes the *Shelby American*. Many regional groups and annual convention.

Ford T-5 Owners Association
c/o Gary Hanson
P.O. Box 808, L-154
Livermore, CA 94550
   Club for owners and enthusiasts of T-5 (Export) Mustangs.

SVT Cobra Owners Association
212 West Iris
McAllen, TX 78501
www.scoa.org
   Club is dedicated to the 1993-up Mustang Cobra.

SVT Cobra Mustang Club
1642 Huntmoor Drive,
Rock Hill, SC 29732
www.svtcobraclub.com
   Club is dedicated to the 1993-up Mustang Cobra.

Index

5.0L GT, 141
5.0LX Convertible Special, 138
390 GT Mustang, 180
428 Mach 1, 66
1964 1/2 Mustang, 11
1965-66 Shelby Mustang, 62
1965 convertible GT, 22
1965 GT 350, 153
1965 Indianapolis 500 Pace Cars, 20
1965 Mustang 11, 146
1965 Shelby Mustang 158, 171
1966 GT 350, 153, 163
1966 Mustang, 10, 23, 25
1966 Shelby Mustang, 163, 166, 171
1967 Mustang, 29
1968 GT350 convertible, 182
1968 Mustang, 37, 40
1968 Mustang Fastback, 206, 208
1969 Boss 302, 56, 68, 82
1969 Boss 429, 56
1969 Mach 1, 188
1969 Mustang, 47
1969 Mustang GT, 55
1969 Shelby Mustang 55, 188
1970 Boss 302, 77
1970 Boss 429, 79, 81
1970 Mach 1, 94
1970 Mustang, 68
1971 Boss 351, 99
1971 Grande, 88
1971 Mustang, 83, 183
1972 Mustang, 97
1973 Mustang, 101, 103, 104
1974 Mustang II, 101, 104
1979 Mustang, 120
1979 Mustang Pace Car, 122
1982 Mustang GT, 126
1985 Mustang, 133
1985 Mustang GT, 131
1986 Mustang, 133
1987 GT, 134
1987 Mustang GT, 127
1988 GT, 134

1989 GT, 134
1990 Mustang, 137
1993 Cobra, 138
1993 Mustang R, 205, 207
1994 Boss, 192
1994 Cobra, 192
1994 Cobra GT, 192
1994 Mustang, 147, 148, 192
1994 Pace Car convertible, 191, 192
1995 Cobra convertible, 190
1995 Cobra R, 150
1995 Mustang R, 205, 207
1996 Cobra, 195–199
1996 Mustang ,194
1996 Mustang GT convertible, 194
1997 Mustang, 199
1997 Mustang GT, 199
1997 Mustang GT Sport Group, 200
1998 Cobra, 200
1999 Cobra, 203, 204, 206
1999 Cobra R, 206
1999 Mustang 201, 202, 204
1999 Mustang GT, 203
2000 Mustang convertible, 208
2000 Mustang GT Coupe, 208
2000 Mustang R, 204, 205, 207
2001 Cobra, 206
2001 Mustang, 206
2001 Mustang Bullitt GT, 207–209
2003 Cobra, 210

Boss 302, 58, 61, 66, 76, 78, 79, 81
Boss 351, 93, 94, 99, 188
Boss 351 Mustang, 97
Boss 429, 46, 61, 62, 65, 66, 82, 151, 196
Boss Mustang, 149

Cobra 139, 149
Cobra II 111, 113–115

Cobra Mustang, 121
Cobra R 139, 151, 152
Cobra R Mustangs, 139

Ghia, 110
GL, 128
GLX, 128
Grande, 46, 52, 74, 103, 110
GT 53, 137, 139, 149
GT350, 164, 174, 180, 187
GT350H, 169
GT500, 11, 174, 177, 178, 180, 183, 187, 188, 191
GT500KR, 183

Hemi Charger (1968), 209

King Cobra, 114, 115

L, 128
Lincoln Mark VIII, 197, 205
LX, 137
LX Mustang, 134

Mach 1, 46, 53, 54, 66, 68, 71, 74, 88, 91, 99, 103, 115, 149, 188
McLaren Mustang, 126
Mustang E, 52
Mustang GT, 74, 128, 129

Outlaw XS, 142

SAAC MK I, 141, 142
SAAC MK II, 141, 142
SAAC Snake, 141
Saleen Mustang, 136, 198, 200
Shelby Mustangs, 193
Sprint 200, 27
Steeda GT 140, 141

Turbo Mustang GT, 129